CLAIRE,
THANKS FOR
YOUR SUPPORT.
HOPE YOU
ENJOY!

SELLING TO MEN

SELLING TO WOMEN

D1282275

The Significant Impact of Gender Communication

In The Selling Process

SELLING TO MEN

SELLING TO WOMEN

A New Sales Philosophy for the Twenty-First Century

For free downloads of sales forms and more information on

Selling to Men and Selling to Women

go to: www.ywomen.biz

Selling To Men, Selling to Women

Copyright © 2005 *Fushian LLC*

ISBN: 0-9770855-8-9

5th Printing: January 2014

Published By:
Fushian, LLC d/b/a YWomen
320 Thorndale Court
Roswell, GA 30075
www.ywomen.biz

All rights reserved. No part of this book may be reproduced, stored in a retrieval system, or transmitted by any means, electronic, mechanical, photocopying, recording, or otherwise, without written permission from the author.

Printed in the United States of America

Table of Contents

Dedications

Jeffery

To the most important people in my life, my wife Phyllis, my children Heather and Jeff Jr., and to my mother Jeanne.

Gillian

To Lauren, the daughter who taught me what selling and gender are all about!

Acknowledgements

This is a book about selling and being a salesman. As a salesman, I have had the pleasure to work with and learn from some of the best people in the many industries, and though I have lost touch with many of them, my hope is they will pick up this book and give me a call. To Jim Hargraves and Dean Milo, who encouraged a pushy kid from Wisconsin. To my business partners, first Gary Priem and later Mike deJulien. I learned a lot from both of you.

To Dave Kirkpatrick, the best salesman I have *ever* met. To my Sales Mentor Rick Morgan and to all the gang in Chicago including Jim Browning, Mike Carroll, Bill Deakin, Jaci Fox, Tony Hise, David Kennedy, Chris Meis, Leon Lane, Tai Lynch, Tim Pirrung, Jack Reeder, Carl Sweat, Joe Szombathy, Mike Wilson, and Bernie Ward; absolutely the best sales group ever assembled.

I would also like to thank all the folks in 'Indy' who really taught me the true nature of relational selling. Tony Stroinski, Kirk Freese, Matt Carrico, John Dougherty, Terri Reilly, Ken Miklos and especially Bill Marty, who coined the sales line, *'find out what they want and give it to them'.*

I'd also like to thank the folks I had the pleasure of working with in Customer Marketing; especially Steve Horgan, Steve Kelly, Ann Nicholas, Mike Mapes, Nate Papillion, Roberta Spiess, John O'Flaherty, Bill Overend, Stennis Shotts, Dave Snyder, Bob Tufts, Lori Wilkinson, Jeff

Weekley, and especially Paul Murphy for always pushing for the *greatest* sales presentation of all time.

This book is about being a salesman, but it's also about being a passionate champion of workplace diversity and leadership development. I want to thank Liz Freedman for starting me on this journey and my two life coaches Tricia Brennesholtz and Meg Altenderfer for helping guide me on this path.

I also want to thank the other incredible people who have supported me in this work including Lori Addicks, Nadia Bilchik, Tony Brown, Cade Cowan, Alyson Daichendt, Jane Finchum, Ed Gadsden, Jennifer Hale, Robbie Houcek, Julie Hamilton, Rena Holland, Melanie Miller, Bronwyn Morgan, Maryellen O'Neill, Juli Shook, Mary Anne Sirotko-Turner, Susan zumBrunnen, Jerry Wilson, and the incredible Nancy Wollensak-Gilboe. You are special friends.

I also want to thank Karen Hendrix, Valerie Usilton and Carolyn Jackson for supporting me in my career and allowing me to do this work while keeping my day job.

Additional thanks go out to people who supported me in bringing this book to print. Molly Epstein of Emory University and Spring Asher of Georgia Tech for their contributions on gender and communications. To Connie Glaser and Michelle Byrne, for their advice and encouragement. To Fred Schwab, Greg Sinatra and Bob Facazio for their 'men's' perspectives on a host of sales related issues and to Charlie Brock for introducing me to Gillian Royes, without whom I could not have written this book.

Finally to my dear friends Daphne Schechter, John Byrne and Steve Flaim. Your encouragement, support and friendship are priceless. Thanks for everything!

Jeffery Tobias Halter

Preface

The world does not need another book on selling!

This was my thought 32,000 feet over the Arizona desert. I was returning from a Gender Differences conference and about all I learned in the previous two days was that men and women communicate differently. This was not new news to me. I had been working in diversity education and strategy at a Fortune 50 company for over five years, but, as I thought back on my career, it dawned on me that this was new news for many people… many SALESpeople.

You see, before moving into diversity strategy and education, I had been a salesman. For over 20 years I sold everything from cosmetics to diapers to multi-million dollar cooperative marketing programs. I dealt with virtually every major grocery chain in the country. I was a certified trainer in three different sales technologies. I even won a new car at the age of 24 for being the number one salesmen in the country. Sales was my life, and I have a library full of sales books to prove it.

I have facilitated sales training for thousands of people. I have taught an undergraduate business communication course and have evaluated graduate level MBAs on their communication skills -- yet I have never ever heard anyone talk about gender differences in the sales area.

The world does not need another book on selling!

As this thought kept ringing in my head, I started to think about this fact: the ability to communicate is the most vital skill a salesperson can possess. The ability to listen, to determine buying needs, to move the sales process forward, to sell the benefits of goods and services, to handle objections, to close – all of the elements depend on communication skills.

This is hardly new news to the professional salesperson. Literally thousands of books have been written on how to communicate, and thousands more on how to sell. But something has always been missing. Sales books focus on selling: a five-step process, a seven-step process, economic buyer, power buyer, sales cycle, customer relationship management, handling objectives, 15 different closing techniques. Every selling technology talks endlessly about buyers, and what and how they buy. Yet one extremely important variable in selling today is seldom, if ever, discussed.

The most significant variable in every sales situation is the gender of the buyer, and more importantly, how the salesperson communicates to the buyer's gender. It is now a validated and documented fact that men and women communicate differently, very differently. Everything from eye contact, to body language, to the usage of language to the processing of information is different in men and women.

Does the world need another book on selling?

This may sound obvious, but chances are now at least 50/50 that, if you're in sales, you will be selling to a man or selling to a woman. This varies widely by industry; however, we seldom talk about how we need to communicate differently to these buyers. We've had books on general sales processes, books on marketing to men and women, but nothing that addresses a technique for sales or the sales process; and whether you sell pharmaceuticals, computers or real estate, men and women communicate differently and consequently need to be sold to differently.

Additionally, if you sell the three most important items that people buy in their lifetime – their house, their car, and their financial services and insurance – you are usually selling to a man and a woman at the same time. Each has different buying habits, motivations and needs. In today's environment, you'd better be prepared to handle all of these.

Maybe the world needs another book on selling!

This book is written for sales professionals: salesmen and saleswomen. This means you have chosen sales as a career. If you are a good salesperson, I know you want to get better. If you're an excellent sales professional, hopefully you are making a comfortable six-figure salary. Chances are you are a male. My estimate is that over 90 percent of salespeople who are making over $100,000 a year are men. My research indicates that fewer than 15 books have been written on selling to women, not marketing to, but how to sell to them. Most of the women who wrote these books were not sales professionals, but gender communication specialists. They may be the perfect person to write a book on communications, but they aren't salespeople. They don't make their living building relationships and bringing creative solutions to people to satisfy their needs. Sales people do that.

The world needs another book on selling!

Almost two years after this first thought, I had the pleasure of meeting Gillian Royes, a diversity consultant specializing in gender issues. She had already written one book on the subject called *Sexcess: The New Gender Rules at Work,* and she told me this book had to be written. We were both aware of the tremendous changes taking place in this country's work life and marketplace, and that few people were addressing that issue.

Together we have created a program and, yes, another book on selling intended to guide male and female salespeople through the expanding minefield of selling to the different genders and responding satisfactorily to their concerns. The EVOLVE Tool and the Evolved Selling Model are the result of my many years of experience in sales and our combined knowledge of the rapidly changing social environment in this country and overseas.

The world needs another book on selling!

Change is a good thing, it's said, but understanding change and being prepared for it is even better. Just as *Who Moved My Cheese?* by Spencer Johnson and Kenneth H. Blanchard told a simple and yet powerful story about change management, my hope is that this book will do the same for sales. *Selling to Men, Selling to Women,* written by a man with the assistance of a woman, is as unbiased as we could make it. We constantly checked each other if we felt that we were bashing either gender. What we wanted to do was tell the hard truth about what each gender specifically needs to observe and practice in order to close that sale to either a male or a female client. And now...

The world has one more book on selling!

Introduction

"Amazing! In over 30 years of selling I never thought about it!"

Bob Focazio is a 35-year sales veteran. As national sales manager for AT&T, he has managed over 9,000 sales people and the company's Sales School. I believe Bob to be typical of most sales people and sales trainers. When Bob Focazio said, "I never thought about it!", I knew it was time to write a book. Bob agreed with me that, yes, men and women communicate differently, but, no, it has never been taught in any sales school.

Gender was not discussed in the past and, as a result, the sales game and sales training have not really changed in the past 30 years. On the surface it seems so obvious a change, even simple… and yet it is so complicated.

Men and Women Communicate Differently, VERY Differently

In the past few years, millions of dollars of research have been done on gender brain functions, speech patterns, body language, listening skills, and the list goes on and on. So why is this so important today and why is it really important for salespeople? It's because we are communicators, and great salespeople are great communicators. Now I'm not talking about order takers, or the salesman who sold you your carpeting and had the sales skills of Krusty the Clown.

Most great salespeople are good at listening, are adaptable, and truly want to bring you a successful solution to your problem. Selling today is moving from the transactional steps of yesterday to relationship-based value selling. Selling and the selling game is actually changing gender. This might be uncomfortable to some people, but we'll show you what's going on and why the game is changing.

How to Read This Book

I don't know about you, but I can't recall the last book I read cover to cover. My goal is for you to very quickly find what you need to be more successful, go out and practice these skills, and then return to this book as needed to hone your new found skills.

Part One examines the business case for a new approach to selling and the urgent need to do things differently. Part Two discusses current sales processes and the impact that gender has on the way you sell. Part Three provides you with the tools you will need to use to be successful in the new world of sales.

Throughout the book we will give you data to consider. Data about selling. Data about the changing marketplace. Data about the changing workplace. Data about communication skills. We will explore the changing climate of the entire sales profession. We will look at who is buying "stuff" and who is selling "stuff" and we'll explore gender differences on the scientific and social levels. For our hard data, we have omitted stating a source for each fact, but we have used the U.S. Census Bureau and Department of Labor statistics for 2000 to 2005, along with sources like Catalyst, the working women's research organization, and scientific research websites. Our secondary sources came from professional organizations' websites and journals, sales books, and gender publications.

My hope is that you will question some of what you read and do not take it at face value. I encourage you to do more research on the topic of gender communications as this will only deepen your understanding of the topic. To help you in your search please refer to the list of topics in the Bibliography.

As you read our book, you will see that most of the comments about gender differences are written as generalized statements (i.e., women do this, men do that). It is important for you to know that these statements are true in the majority of cases. When we say that men use fewer words than women, we mean that research has shown that about 80 percent of the time it's true, and yet we all know some men who can outtalk women.

When we say that women are into the relationship component of buying and selling, we know that about 80 percent of the time it's true. Yet I have sold to many women who only cared about price, product and delivery, and did not care about a relationship with our company. We all know men who love to shop and women who hate it. It is this ability to switch roles that makes sales so challenging, and why it is so important for salespeople to understand where the client is coming from at all points.

It is these majority research findings about both genders that make this book particularly meaningful, because at any given time in the sales process you will need to remember that the odds are 80:20 that the man or woman in front of you belongs to that 80 percent that tends to have certain traits and behaves in a certain way. And you will also be observing to see if the traits and behaviors belong to the other 20 percent. With that knowledge, you will be able to use the tools and selling process that we are providing.

Part One of the book is designed to help you with a basic understanding of gender differences and communications. You'll get a gender quiz that, when honestly answered, will let you know just how "male" or "female" you are in your behavior and feelings. To get you thinking outside of your gender box, we'll give you simple exercises at the end of Chapters 1, 2 and 3 called **Try This On**. These are fun and challenging exercises that will not only get you thinking about what is important for the opposite gender, but will also be great conversation points at your next training meeting.

In Part Two, we'll be looking at sales processes both old and new. We'll examine the way men and women currently sell, typically using either a transactional or relational model. We'll examine these models and look at their strengths and weaknesses. We'll also look at the challenge of selling to men and women at the same time. And then, if you're man (or woman) enough, we will give you one more sales process to try.

In Part Three we'll share a new selling philosophy - the Evolved Selling Model, the EVOLVE Tool, and the Evolved Selling Process - which combines the Model and the Tool. When properly executed, the Tool can be used at any time while selling, and will help you evolve any sale to any customer making the customer satisfied and yourself richer in the process. We will give you the necessary templates to become more effective in utilizing your newly learned skills.

So to get us started, we have said men and women communicate differently; now let's begin to explore why this is such a big deal for everyone in the twenty-first century, especially salespeople.

Part One

Chapter 1
The Perfect Storm

> "It would be a disaster of epic proportions! It would be the perfect storm!"
> - A weatherman in the movie *The Perfect Storm*

America is becoming the world's most diverse country. The changes we will see in demographics in the next 35 years will be more significant than our country has witnessed in **all** of its first 235 years. We are changing in numbers, in minority representation, in culture. These changes will not only be seen on Main Street, but also on Wall Street.

Talk to any business leader today, in virtually any industry, and they will tell you that the greatest challenge they have is attracting, developing and retaining a highly skilled workforce.

The impending labor force challenges that are coming in the United States create - The Perfect Storm! As recently as 1980, the total number of minorities in the work force (other than women), represented just 20%. This number will explode to 50% in the next 35 years.

At the same time, Baby Boomers who have had far fewer children themselves will lead to a slowing in the supply of workers. As Boomers start to leave the work force, the very nature of work and the market place itself will begin to change.

Exactly what does this mean? Fushian, a consulting group, uses the visual on the next page (by no means scientific) to depict the coming crisis.

Beginning on January 1, 2008, 60 percent of the Prime Work Force (PWF, also known as Boomers), primarily white males, will be able to retire. This represents 10,000 workers per day leaving the workforce. As of 2005, of the people entering the workforce, a minimum of 75 percent will be women and minorities (W+M).

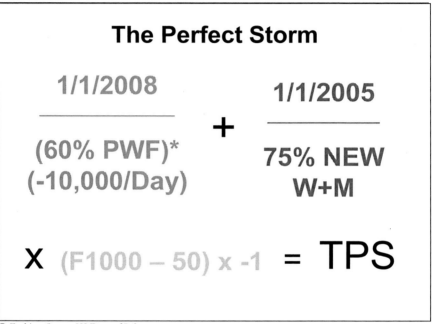

© Fushian, Source US Dept of Labor.

It is anticipated that, beginning in 2008, women and minorities will flood management ranks as the PWF retires. Even with the employment slowdown recently, the Bureau of Labor Statistics says that employment will grow about 14 percent in the next 10 years.

The result will be a tremendous drain in corporate knowledge, a massive influx of talent that looks and acts differently than its predecessors and every company in America fighting for the best and brightest individuals.

Selling to Men Selling to Women

In the figure (F1000 – 50) represents the 950 Companies in the Fortune 1000 that don't get it! These 950 companies that do not begin in the engagement, recruitment and retention of activities targeted toward women and minorities will be left behind. According to Diversity Inc, the web-based diversity research firm, only about 50 companies really 'get it' and they have put significant efforts into managing diverse workforces.

The (–1) that ends the equation represents the negative impact of this situation. This equation of workplace departures plus a vastly different workforce multiplied by a fight for talent equals - The Perfect Storm!

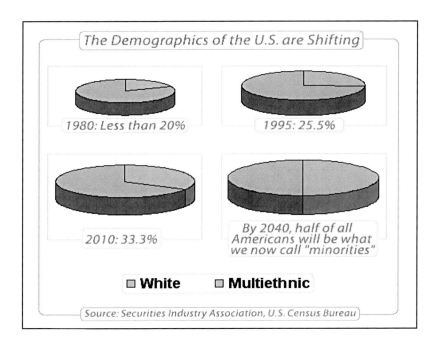

In very real terms, the Bureau of Labor Statistics calculates that the resulting shortage will be about 10 million workers. This gap will continue to grow by almost 1,000,000 per year until technology is able to replace many positions.

If you're a salesperson you'd better evolve quickly, because all of the order-taker jobs will soon be replaced by the Internet and a few microchips.

Marketing is Starting to Get it

As demonstrated in The Perfect Storm, business and human resources will soon be forced to keep up with the dazzling speed of change in minority dominance, workforce numbers, four generations of people at work, gays and lesbians out of the closet, and empowered disabled workers. Marketing and advertising have observed these trends and are now moving into position to address them.

> ### U.S. Minority Buying Power
>
> By 2008, the combined buying power (i.e. disposable income), of African Americans, Hispanics, Asian Americans and Native Americans will exceed $1.5 trillion, more than triple the 1990 level of $456 billion. That's a gain of $1.1 trillion, or 231 percent.
>
> This is also roughly equal to the economy of Mexico.
>
> *-The Multicultural Economy: Minority Buying Power in the New Century*

For example, my old employer Proctor and Gamble has created a Multicultural Business Development Organization that focuses on marketing to Hispanics all over the world. Other US companies including Johnson and Johnson, AT&T and Toyota, have found out that Asian Americans are incredibly brand loyal and have been spending millions on marketing to that group.

Mercedes-Benz USA is doing the same with targeted African American advertising. They know that this consumer group is predicted to reach $852 billion by 2007.

Another emerging market that has surprised the pundits with its rapid growth is that of gays and lesbians. Buying power for this market is projected to reach $608 billion by 2007. The travel industry has awakened to the fact that this consumer segment loves to vacation and spends lavishly to do so. Given that most partnered couples do not have children, their level of disposable income is significantly higher than the rest of the population.

Gays and Lesbians
- 85% percent of gays and lesbians, for example, took a vacation in the last year, compared to 64 % of mainstream customers.
- 58% of Fortune 500 Companies now offer Same-Sex Partner benefits.

-Diversity Inc. October 2004

Marketing departments in corporations across the country are not waiting for exact figures. They have seen the projected purchasing power of women, minorities and gays and they are acting on that knowledge. They are not only marketing directly at these formerly hidden customers, but they are creating products specially for these new markets, such as SUVs with lower access and extra mirrors to keep an eye on the kids in the back, and cruises designed for gay singles and couples.

Marketers know that there's big money to be made from women. Advertising agencies are using creative women to come up with ads for their clients that are directed straight at the hearts and minds of women. Gender differences have become a big part of their appeal. There's even a women's magazine advertisement for Harley Davidson motorcycles that simply says, "It vibrates." Off the wall and definitely edgy. Would a man have thought of that – or dared to do it? Cutting edge marketing understands exactly what's happening in the country and goes for it. As this is a book on the significant role of gender in selling, let's explore deeper the exploding trend of women's buying power.

The Changing Marketplace – Women Buy Everything!

Women are the primary purchasers of ... damn near everything. We must, therefore, strive to achieve nothing less than total enterprise realignment around this awesome, burgeoning, astoundingly untapped market.
- Tom Peters
Re-Imagine! Business Excellence in a Disruptive Age

If you don't understand the major changes going on in the American marketplace at this very moment, and if the facts you've just read don't signal something vitally different from the old way of doing business, it's time for you to consider moving out of sales.

Consider this fact:

> In the United States, women make 85% of consumer purchases and influence over 95% of total goods & services.
> *-Women & Diversity WOW! FACTS 2004*

And that's not all. In addition to women buying most of the household goods in America, women also:

- Own more than half of all stocks.
- Are the fastest growing segments of the home-buying market and account for one-third of all condominium purchases.
- Purchase 65% of all new cars.
- Women owned businesses spend more than $546 billion annually on salaries and benefits.

This is only the tip of the iceberg. Throughout the book you will see references to the enormous purchasing power of women. Why is this important? Well, we're all very good at being in denial as long as possible in order to stay in our comfort zone. This is not the time. Male and female salespeople alike will have to rethink their entire perspective on how business in America is conducted, who buys what, who has power, and how best to approach their new targets. In other words, there has to be a revolution in our sales approach. Why is this important? Because salespeople just don't get it!

The Betrayal of Marketing by Sales!

Marketing gets it. Advertising gets it. But most sales departments don't have a clue! I have heard versions of the following story at least ten times and so I will share it with you to demonstrate the problem of connecting all of the dots. A female customer walks in the door to buy a car, say a Volvo. Looks like easy pickings for a salesperson, right? Not today.

That woman has already seen hundreds of Volvo marketing products: ads in all the media -- TV, radio, magazines, newspapers -- and heard, read and seen all about the safety and comfort features.

She has gone onto the Internet and checked out the Volvo websites, gotten background information including the location of available dealers and the cars in stock. She has spoken to friends who bought Volvos.

> The companies, from Fortune 500s to mom and pops to start-up entrepreneurs, that do the best job of marketing to women will **dominate every significant product and service category.**
>
> -Faith Popcorn, marketing futurist,
> *Eveolution:*
> *The Eight Truths of Marketing to Women*

And, thanks to the Internet, she's even figured out, within a few hundred dollars, what the car should cost.

Volvo's Marketing Division has done its job. She knows more about the car than the salesman who greets her at the door. But how is she treated? As if she has a low IQ, is slightly hard of hearing, and really has no right buying a luxury car; however if she brought a male friend with her to the dealer, chances are the clueless salesperson spent most of his time talking to him.

Recently a female friend was so disgusted by how the salesman was treating her that she drove her old Honda out of a Honda dealership and went directly across the street and bought a brand new Toyota.

Just because she liked Hondas it didn't stop her from leaving her brand to join another because of poor customer service. Honda Marketing had done its job, but the salesman let them down. This linkage of women to brands is also of significant importance.

Now I know what your thinking, "I'm a sales professional, not a used car salesmen, how does this apply to me?"

Women Don't Buy Brands; They Join Them

Women join brands. They develop relationships with brands, products and people. According to many relationship-selling advocates, women support women, and the few men who get it.

> Truth No. 1:
> When it comes to women...it's time to **think link**.
> -Faith Popcorn
> *Eveolution The Eight Truths of Marketing to Women*

Women are joiners. They love connecting with people, family, friends, strangers, and they support other women. Is this a biological or learned behavior? Well, it is now known that it is a combination of both, and more biological than we first thought.

Selling to women is different from selling to men because as science has been showing us for the last decade your female client has a different brain and body structure from the male client next to her, PLUS she grew up being treated differently, PLUS she had different experiences as a female. It is for that reason that she buys products and services in a different way from a male customer. These unique physiological and psychological differences will be explored in our next chapter. We will also explore deeper the challenges involved in selling to women if you bring a traditional male viewpoint.

> 89 percent of women say that they will shop at one store over another if the service is better.

If women are now the purchasers of almost everything in America, then as salespeople we need to figure this out. Just as women are loyal to brands and stores, they will also be loyal to the salespeople who really understand them.

We will also discuss women in sales, their strengths and their weaknesses and how their selling skills are different from men, not better, not worse, just different. We will not preach that women need to be more like men, but we will examine the sales process and look at areas that may be hindering women from being as successful as they can be. Why is this important? Because, much as things have changed, men still remain in charge.

Men Still Rule!

Given the sheer numbers and the positions held, men rule business. Consider these facts for a minute:

- Men head 496 of the Fortune 500 companies.
- Men hold 87% of line officer positions.
- 75% of all men are in the labor force, compared to 60% of all women.
- Men continue to dominate in the construction, IT, petrochemical, and automotive sectors among many others.

Is it still a male dominated world? Well in our research you'd never believe the incredible lack of information about men in business. It's because men **are** business today. In order to get our figures, we had to deduct the women's percentages from 100 percent. We began to call men the "default gender" after that! Yet the truth is that while women may control 85 percent of consumer purchases, men clearly control a great majority of business purchasing. It is for this reason that this book is so helpful for women in understanding how to sell to men.

Selling to Men…Price, Product, Pleasure

Women enjoy making fun of men. They seem far too logical, too cold, and too focused on their creature comforts.

However, once women understand how men's brains work, and how this translates to behavior, they will see that men are operating in ways that make a lot of sense to them.

> What's the point of going out? We're just going to wind up back here anyway.
> - Homer Simpson

Understanding these behaviors can help female salespeople to be more effective in selling to men.

Take the sales process, for example. Most men are largely transactional when they buy. How much is it, and what should I know about the product? Men like facts and figures. But the real reason men buy is the same reason women do -- it fulfills a need. Needs are defined in many different ways. In business, purchasing managers are buying things for their company. If they do their job well, the company does well and they are rewarded, (i.e., they receive the pleasure of a paycheck and bonus, and their needs are met).

In *Conceptual Selling*, Robert Miller and Stephen Heiman said it best: "People don't buy a product per se; they buy what the product will do for them." For men, products fill a very functional need. And most sales training and selling books have focused on the transactional process. Beginning as early as 1920, the entire sales industry was about men, and the books that were being written on the sales process did it the man's way (i.e., the transactional way).

Most of these books focused on catchy opening lines and snappy closing techniques and certainly did the traveling salesmen of the day proud. As long as men dominated sales, transactional selling ruled the day, well into the 1990's.

> Linda Lohman: "I just thought you'd like a change…."
> Willy Lohman: "I don't want a change!"
> - Arthur Miller, *Death of a Salesman*

My personal exposure to this started in 1982, when I joined Procter & Gamble as a sales representative in paper products in the very rural Upper

Peninsula of Michigan. I sold toilet paper and diaper displays to little mom and pop stores all across the peninsula.

Procter & Gamble's bible was a five-step process, and you had to follow every step, every time! Twelve calls a day, two presentations per call. On days when my Unit Manager would work with me, I got evaluated on 24 sales presentations. It's said that P & G gives you a million-dollar sales training program; they just shove it down your throat a nickel at a time. In other words, it was painful. Store managers would actually hide when they saw P & G salespeople come into their stores. This was transactional selling at its worst. Of course, we know that those days are gone... or are they?

In Chapter 5 on *Selling to Men*, we will examine the transactional selling model. This chapter was written for two reasons. It shows us how the cultural setting of the day established a sales pattern and process that worked, and gives us a baseline to begin thinking about sales as a professional activity with a model and techniques. The chapter was also written with women in mind to help them better understand the transactional process and examine how some of their strengths as a relationship builder may actually hinder them in their sales effort when the customer is a man.

At the risk of sounding like a doomsday prophet, let me repeat: The Perfect Storm is coming. The workforce and the marketplace are changing at rates that have never been matched in human history. As salespeople we need to evolve or we will become extinct. So how can you evolve?

First, you need to better understand the people you are selling to. Then you need to adapt your sales approach. In order to get started, we need to understand something of the differences between the two genders, validated by recent research studies by the dozen. Any sales process that is going to work with gender needs to have a foundation, and ours is scientific. Read on to learn what you need to know to sell to everyone.

TRY THIS ON:

Determine your own 'Business Case' for The Perfect Storm. Write down how your company has changed in the last 5 years. Ask yourself the following questions:

- How different is my company's product line versus 5 years ago?
- How has the make-up of my customers changed?
- What new or emerging segments have we entered?
- What will the demographics of our company be in the next 5 years?

TRY THIS ON:

Get into the new consumer's mindset. Keep a log of all the major purchases made for a four week period in your household.

- Who was the primary purchaser of each item and what is their gender?
- What influenced the purchaser to make the decision?

LEARNING POINTS FROM THIS CHAPTER

1. Wide-spread diversity is now an established fact in the American workforce.

2. As the Boomer generation begins to retire in 2008, women and minorities will make up 75% of those entering the workforce.

3. Women buy almost everything sold in America outside of business to business.

4. The marketing department understands the changes and are rapidly making adjustments in their marketing activities, unlike the sales function.

5. The sales professional will have to become familiar with the new markets and adapt quickly in order to survive.

Chapter 2
Men and Women Communicate Differently,
VERY Differently

A woman can effortlessly speak 6,000 to 8,000 words a day, use an additional 2,000-3,000 vocal sounds and 8,000-10,000 gestures and body signals. A man utters 2,000-4,000 words, 1,000-2,000 vocal sounds and makes 2,000-3,000 body language signals. **In other words, women communicate three times more than men.** They also suffer from four times the jaw problems as men.

- Barbara and Allan Pease
Why Men Don't Listen and Women Can't Read Maps

This chapter is intended to help you to begin to understand gender differences at a deeper level. My goal is for you to understand that there are physiological and psychological reasons for the differences between men and women. This may be more information than you think you need, but not talking about it would be like just talking about the features and advantages of both genders without providing any proof. You will find that if you understand the causes for gender differences the benefit statements will become very apparent.

A friend said to me, "These are just generalities. There are no facts to support this, are there?" The answer is a decided YES, and to save you time I will summarize for you much of the current research being done in the field. I heartily encourage you to do your own research. Gender differences play out in every minute of our lives from the minute we are born until the minute we die.

As a salesperson, I hope you will read this chapter with great interest, as it will give you knowledge to explore the world of gender and use these new skills to be more effective at work.

Finally, as we will say at least ten times in this book, these statements are true in the majority of cases. These are well researched and well documented studies but as we have said before, not every man or every woman is the same.

What is of interest is that women will read this chapter and get it. You see, women do not see gender as a binary. Women are very comfortable running the gamut of the gender continuum. Men see things as binary, yes/no, black/white, male/female, vertical issues. Women see them as horizontal continuums with lots of gray areas, and they feel very comfortable moving back and forth on the continuum. This is natural and physiological and makes them much more relational. It also allows them to 'try on' male things, (from jobs to clothes) and feel very comfortable doing it.

Feel the Fear and Take the Test

Before we go into any details, we want you to accept a challenge. The test printed on the next page will help you to see where you fall on the male/female spectrum. How male and how female are you? Answer honestly, and you may be surprised by the results.

GENDER TRAITS TEST

On the next page you will find a Gender Traits Test, which is a way of judging just how 'male' or 'female' you are in your behavior and feelings.

Don't over-think your answers; just answer using the scale on the next page.

Answer the questions as to how the term describes you best according to the following scale:

1 = Never or almost never true
2 = Usually not true
3 = Sometimes but infrequently true
4 = Occasionally true
5 = Often true
6 = Usually true
7 = Always or almost always true

Adaptable	Affectionate	Aggressive
Conceited	Compassionate	Assertive
Conventional	Eager to soothe feelings	Defensive of beliefs
Conscientious	Gentle	Dominant
Jealous	Loves children	Forceful
Moody	Sensitive to the needs of others	Has leadership abilities
Reliable	Sympathetic	Independent
Secretive	Tender	Strong personality
Tactful	Understanding	Willing to take a stand
Truthful	Warm	Willing to take risks

GENDER TRAITS TEST SCORING
From the top, total the SECOND and THIRD columns.
(The first column is a control column, and we'll ignore it.)

Total from the SECOND column is Score A:_____

Total from the THIRD column is Score B:_____

Subtract Score A minus Score B for the Difference

Score:_____

Example: if your A score is 90 and your B score is 70,
it would be 90 minus 70 = 20, or plus 20.

If your A score is 70 and your B score is 90,
it would be 70 minus 90 = –20 or minus 20.

GENDER TRAITS SCORES
Masculine –20 and under
Nearly Masculine –19 to –10
Androgynous –9 to +9
Nearly feminine +9 to +19
Feminine +20 and over

Credits:
Bem, S.L., "The Measurement of Psychological Androgyny,"
Journal of Personality and Social Psychology, 1975, Vol. 31.

Of course, this is just a fun, self-administered test and it doesn't prove anything. Or does it? A significant part of this book is focused on being introspective. In Chapter 10, the EVOLVE Tool will ask you to examine any gender bias that you might have. It will ask you to genuinely value the person to whom you're selling. It will challenge you to remain open minded and really listen to your customer. It will ask you to validate facts and then it will ask you to either engage or empathize. Hopefully, this test gives you a little more to think about in terms of your own personality and behavior as part of that process.

Additionally, this chapter will be especially tough for men. While men know that they are obviously different from women, they just don't talk about it. There's a reason for that; men see the world as a set of facts. Men want the facts, just the facts. There's nothing wrong with that, but if you are going to evolve from the transactional world of selling to the relational world of big ticket selling you better be willing to try this on! It's hard and it's uncomfortable. Gender is not binary. It is a continuum, and we need to start to understand this today.

So to get us started here are the facts and the latest scientific research coming from brain scans, endocrinology, and neurology.

The Facts Speak for Themselves

Until the early 1990's, it was thought that all brains were the same. A man's body was known to be different to a woman's in terms of size and strength, but the brain, well, that was the same. Women were just thought to be weak of character or indecisive. Magnetic resonance imaging (MRI) scans changed all of that. Beginning in the late 1980's, this new technology was to revolutionize brain analysis and demonstrate repeatedly that there were certain ways in which the typical man's brain was different from the typical woman's brain. Earlier tests had already established that the left and right brain hemispheres carried out different functions.

Gender Brain Differences

As a result of MRI research into brain activity while men and women were performing language tasks, Drs. Bennett and Shaywitz and their team at Yale University found in 1995 that men use mainly the left brain for speech tasks and women use both the left and right. Women later research showed, switch routinely between both brain hemispheres.

LEFT AND RIGHT BRAIN FUNCTIONS

LEFT BRAIN FUNCTIONS	RIGHT BRAIN FUNCTIONS
uses logic	uses feeling
detail oriented	"big picture" oriented
facts rule	imagination rules
words and language	symbols and images
present and past	present and future
math and science	philosophy & religion
can comprehend	can get the real meaning
knowing	believing
acknowledges	appreciates
order/pattern perception	spatial perception
knows object name	knows object function
reality based	fantasy based
forms strategies	presents possibilities
practical	impetuous
safe	risk taking

Billions of dollars of scientific research later, we know what our ancestors have always known: men and women are different and nature made it so. As we know, all embryos are female until acted on by a Y chromosome.

With it, the male Y chromosome brings other biological triggers, one of them being brain formation. The main brain difference between men and

For men, language is most often just in the left brain hemisphere, but most women are able to use both sides of the brain for language.

This means that women can communicate up to three times more information than men in the same period of time, speak in more complex patterns, and use longer words.

women, say the researchers, is that the male fetal brain pours testosterone into the baby's body, triggering all kinds of reactions and making the boy different from a female for the rest of his life. It's the testosterone that determines that the baby boy's brain is constructed differently from the baby girl's.

> It is reported that a woman's brain has a larger corpus collusum, which means women can transfer data between the right and left hemisphere faster than men. Men tend to be more left brained, while women have greater access to both sides.

You've probably observed in your own or other people's children that there are certain behaviors that are different in boys and girls.

Girl infants tend to talk earlier than boys, for example, and love the bonding process with their parent. Boy children are more physically energetic and aggressive. How they react to frustrating situations is also different. When a researcher separated one-year-old boys and girls from their mother with a barrier, the boys tried to knock the barrier down while the girls stood there and cried. By the time they reach school age, we see that boys, by and large, are better at tasks requiring spatial skills, and girls at language skills.

The Nature versus Nurture argument has not been completely settled. Do we bring up boys to be aggressive and girls to be nurturing? Whether intended or not, in many ways we continue to have confirmation that there are definite brain and hormonal differences.

> Even though a man has 4% more brain cells, a woman has more connections between brain cells, allowing her to access her emotional/intuitive side faster than a man. The extra brain cells and the greater use of the left brain allow men greater focus on one activity.
>
> Women who accuse men of not listening are merely unaware that men are keenly focused on something other than listening.

Psychological Differences

It's been said that women feel and men act. Let's see what science has to say. Research on emotional intelligence in thousands of men and women found that women, on average, are more aware of their emotions, show more empathy, and are more adept interpersonally. Males are more aggressive than females; young males engage in more rough-and-tumble play than females, and young females are more nurturing.

Men deal with stress much differently than women. Women find it harder to shut down their stress response and become more anxious. They tend to get more depressed than men, although men commit suicide more often than women.

Women really do have intuition, sort of.

A woman's optical receptors are more spread out on the back of her eyes (men's are clustered together for better focus), allowing them to take in more visual images.

Additionally, females have a more acute sense of smell and hearing (which are likely to have developed from an evolutionary need for the mother to recognize and care for her young).

So in fact women's intuition is nothing more than the fact that they are taking in and processing more points of data, and making conclusions based on them.

Women's increased ability to bond and be connected to others explains why women are typically the primary caretakers for children, and increasingly in today's society there own parents.

With the exception of some tiny groups in Asia and Africa, there is no society on earth where men are primary caretakers for children.

In other words, men and women are constructed differently, and they think, feel, and behave differently. So now we know that our brains, bodies, emotions, perceptions, abilities, responses are all different.

But do We Communicate Differently?

The short answer is yes, and it's almost all the time, every day, and everywhere. We opened this chapter with a quote which stated that women communicate three times more than men.

This quote is from a fascinating book by Barbara and Allan Pease called *Why Men Don't Listen and Women Can't Read Maps*, and it supports just what you always suspected. Women run rings around men in the amount of communication area. A woman talks when she's happy, peaceful, angry, anxious… or whatever.

> Men have better logic skills; women have better language skills

Most men are just the opposite. Men tend to either keep their thoughts to themselves more, or not have the thoughts at all.

As far as content is concerned, do men and women communicate the same way? Psychologist John Gray, who wrote that America-boggling book, *Men are from Mars, and Women are from Venus*, declared loudly that each gender speaks its own language.

Based on years of research and experience, Gray summed it up this way:

Men talk to exchange information.	Women talk to express feelings.
Men like to help women by fixing problems.	Women like to help men by improving them.
Men do not like women's attempt to improve them. They feel humiliated.	Women want men to listen to their complaints, not solve them.
When men are down, they want women's loving acceptance, not their criticism and unsolicited advice. Men want to be trusted and admired.	When women are down, they like to talk about their problems. They want men to be sympathetic listeners, not problem solvers.
Men need to be alone sometimes, especially when under stress, and need to retreat to their "cave".	Women, under stress and otherwise, like to seek out contact and make human connections.

Soon after Gray came out with his book, Deborah Tannen, a linguistics expert, wrote about men and women in the American workplace in her book *Talking From 9 to 5*.

Tannen's entire book deals with all of the communication differences between the genders, one of them being something as simple as conversation. She found that men tended to joke, tease, put each other down, and challenge each other just for the sake of the challenge.

> Due to their larger limbric brain, women are more in touch with their feelings, as such they are better able to express them than men.

Women found ways to maintain equality with the other people in the conversation, downplaying their own successes, and enquiring about others' ideas and opinions.

Tannen also found in her research that:

Men and women interpret the same words differently.
- Men equate listening, for example, with getting the results they desire. "She listened to me, and now we have the new system in place."
- Women, on the other hand, think of listening as simply giving the other person an opportunity to share.

Men and women interpret questions differently.
- Asking a person what they think often signals to a man that the questioner has no thoughts of her or his own.
- To a woman, asking what another person thinks is a way of opening the way for discussion and expansion.

Women and men interpret apologies differently.
- Women see apologies as restoring balance.
- Men see apologies as admitting guilt.

Ten thousand neurologists, endocrinologists, psychologists and linguists can't all be wrong. The genders are different, different, different. Once we thought it was only our environment that made us different. Men and women acted like men and women because they were trained at home and school. Now we know, beyond any shadow of a doubt, that our biology makes us different to begin with, and how we're brought up just adds to our gender identity and our behavior toward the other gender.

What science is proving is that it's a good thing that we're different. Let's deal with what we've got, and we'll see that everybody wins and nobody loses. In other words, let's accept the facts and work with them.

So what does this have to do with sales? Well, just about everything!

In our next few chapters we will explore why this is so important. We will examine the enormous purchasing power of women in this country and show how men absolutely do not know how to sell to them. We will then look at the current state of business today and examine how women can be more effective in selling to men. Finally, we will look at one of the most common dynamics of our daily lives, namely, how do you sell to men and women at the same time?

TRY THIS ON:

Go back and review your results from the Gender Traits Test. Look at the areas where you scored a '1'. Examine your own experiences around this, and try practicing just the opposite behavior for one day. See how it feels and how others respond to you. Then try it in a sales situation and see how it feels. It will probably be uncomfortable, but growth and change often are.

TRY THIS ON:

In your next meeting, observe the differences in communication between the women and men present. Ask yourself the following:

- Who talks more, the men or the women?
- Who uses more gestures, men or women?
- What tone of voice do the women and men use most often?
- Which gender seems to dominate, and why?

LEARNING POINTS FROM THIS CHAPTER

1. Gender differences are real and science is proving it.

2. Male and female brains are different in important ways that affect their attitudes and behaviors.

3. Men and women typically communicate differently.

4. Women communicate three times more than men.

5. Women enjoy connecting with other people, whether they're under stress or not. Men often need to withdraw in order to resolve problems.

6. Social scientists and communication experts agree that men and women interpret words, questions and apologize differently.

Chapter 3
Selling to Anyone... Today and Tomorrow

> Personal selling is very labor intensive. That's why it's the most costly way to communicate with prospects. This is its single biggest weakness. A business-to-business sales call today costs well in excess of $300. Not only that, it's very time consuming... (and) the salesperson has incredible power to either make or break a delicate relationship.
>
> - William F. Arens from *Contemporary Advertising*

Once hiring a salesperson was an unavoidable part of doing business. Today we have to face the truth -- the sales professional is becoming dispensable. Advertising is cheaper per customer, and the Internet is a much cheaper and safer alternative. Internet catalog sales are climbing dramatically, and websites give the same information that many sales people can and more. If you don't believe that things are changing in the sales field, consider just this one example:

> Dell Computers sells almost all of its products exclusively over the Internet, without any salespeople calling on its customers. In 2000, the company broke an industry record by selling $50 million PER DAY in Internet sales exclusively. By 2001 it was the leading computer firm in the world.

I'm sure you've gotten a reality check in your own field. To be in the career of sales now means to sharpen your interpersonal communication skills to make you excel over and above any website or competition. Order takers cannot survive under these conditions.

Sales professionals, as expensive as they are within the marketing function, will have to give value to their company, as well as to the customer. In order to do this, he or she will have to dig deeper to satisfy the customer – whether by learning Spanish, reading up on gender research, or personally investigating the benefits of the competitor's product. The alternative is that you will be replaced by a microchip.

Adaptability will determine who gets the job of flying to Tokyo and who doesn't. Being able to work and sell in other cultures in other languages is going to become a super-asset. For men, it's going to be vital to sell to women who won't accept being patronized or ignored. For women, it will be learning how to adopt certain behaviors more comfortable to male clients. For all salespeople, the first new skill will be to learn flexibility in dealing with both genders and be equally comfortable with either.

To begin the process, let's take a deeper look at some of the data discussed in Chapter 1 on each gender in American business today.

Men Still Rule Business!

Women may communicate way more than men, but they're still playing a catch-up game in large businesses - with a long way to go. As of October 2004, men head all but four of the Fortune 500 companies, and they hold 87 percent of corporate officer positions. Men's salaries are more than one and a half times greater than women's, averaging $55,000 for men to a woman's $31,400. A man is three times more likely to earn over $75,000 per year than woman.

Not only are men in charge of most corporations, but in just about every industrial sector men are the primary buyers, controlling major purchasing power in the Aviation, Aerospace, Agriculture, Arms and Ammunition, and Automobile industries. And that's just the start of the alphabet.

Men controlled the bulk of the $10.98 trillion GDP that ran the U.S. in 2003. Men are the leading power in the world in petroleum, steel, motor vehicles, aerospace, telecommunications, chemicals, electronics, and food processing. With expenditures of $2.05 trillion in those industries, we can safely say that men are buying a lot of goods and services in this country and elsewhere. For women working in these sectors you need to be keenly aware of the buying habits of men. Any way you cut it, men are still in charge. Now for another reality check.

Women Find Their Power

American females now form a powerhouse in the US labor force. Consider this:

- Women make up 46% of the labor force in America.
- By 2010, the number of women in the US labor force will have increased by almost 10 million, a growth rate almost one-third higher than for men.
- Nearly three-quarters of all mothers are in the labor force. Even among mothers with young children, 70% work outside the home.

Very few salesmen realize that, slowly but steadily, women are changing the profile of who not only work in, but control business in America.

On the corporate scene for starters:

- Women hold 49.5% of all managerial positions at Fortune 500 companies.
- Women hold 12.5% of corporate officer positions.

54 of the Fortune 500 companies report a woman as their top earner. Brand new research coming out of Catalyst finds that women in high positions in Fortune 1000 companies are just as ambitious as men in wanting that corner office.

Hitting the ceiling on the way there, however, is part of the reality for many women. Not willing to relinquish their roles in business, more and more women have opted out of corporate life and into their own businesses. In fact, what was once a mere trickle has become a flood of women starting their own businesses.

If you don't believe that women's firms are helping to power the economy, read what the Center for Women's Business Research said in 2004:

- Nearly half of the 10.6 million privately-held firms in this country are at least 50% owned by a woman or women.
- Between 1997 and 2004, the estimated growth rate in the number of women-owned firms was nearly twice that of all firms (+17% vs. +9%), and employment expanded at twice the rate of all firms (+24% vs. +12%).
- In 2004, women-owned businesses spent an estimated $546 billion annually on salaries and benefits ($492 billion on salaries and $54 billion for employee benefits – heath, retirement, and insurance).

For salespeople selling to business, here are some more key facts:

- Annual expenditures by women-owned enterprises for just four areas – information technology ($38 billion), telecommunications ($25 billion), human resources services ($23 billion), and shipping ($17 billion) – are estimated to be $103 billion.
- Between 1997 and 2004, privately-held 50% or more women-owned firms diversified into all industries, with the fastest growth in construction (+30% growth), transportation, communications and public utilities (+28% growth), and agricultural services (+24% growth).

Women are holding managerial positions, starting their own companies at an unprecedented rate, and spending money, lots of it. If you think the purchasing power of women in business is mind boggling, let's reexamine more aspects of the purchasing power of women in consumer goods.

Female Buying Power

> David Powers Homes research indicates nearly 80 percent of the home-buying decisions in its price range ($180,000's to $500,000's) are made by women.

Most industries have started doing their own research into this awesome market.

In Chapter 1 we looked at the automobile industry. Here are some more very compelling numbers for just this segment:

- Women represent 50% of total Internet users.
- 80% of women car shoppers get ALL their automotive information online.
- 89% of women are somewhat involved or completely in control of their car's maintenance and service.

The surprises continue to come in, the latest ones being that women buy more sport shoes than men, and they open most of the bank accounts in this country.

Whatever industry you're selling for, chances are that there's a woman either buying from you directly, or influencing the purchase, even if it's the male Purchasing Manager's Assistant. Even within that bastion of male dominance, the Commercial Purchasing profession, women are slowly making strides, moving from the buyer to the managerial level. In 2004, 26 percent of women in that field were purchasing managers, and 1.2 percent were vice presidents. It's also becoming more common for women to become materials managers. There seems to be no buying corner where women are not expanding their presence.

In Chapter 1, we talked about the buying process of men. Let's now take the same opportunity and understand the buying process that's driving the tremendous numbers that are detailed above.

How Women Buy

Modern women make their consumer purchases differently from their mothers, and definitely differently from their grandmothers. Today they use a plethora of resources, from the Internet to mass media to personal shoppers. They do their own research on major purchases like a car, a home or financial services, and they surf the web to comparison shop and make sure they get the best deal.

Time is energy for women today. Women and working women in particular, have turned up the accelerator on many buying transactions today and this is what makes it so challenging to sell to them.

All of that research time reading ads and scanning websites, together with a tighter schedule, work deadlines, and children to be picked up, means that there are times (often frequently) when women become transactional buyers. This is particularly true when they know exactly what they want to buy or are pressed for time.

In one day alone, December 6, 2003, the Home Shopping Network broke a retail sales record by grossing $30 million in TV and web sales – almost entirely from women.

Often they will be saying, just give me what I asked for and let me get out of here.

When this time crunch meets "relational" women, it means as salespeople we have to respond immediately by building that relationship -- or she will be gone. This is true in a grocery store or in a buyer's office.

Does that mean that relationship selling is on the way out? No, it doesn't. There will be times when a woman will carve out time for such traditional relationship selling experiences, mostly because it relaxes her and gives her a chance to interact and communicate. And there will be times when she's not sure about what she wants to buy and needs to get into the conceptual buying mode. She will, at those times, enjoy the process of talking about what she needs, the familiar dance of developing rapport, and the chance to express herself freely and get honest answers in return.

Even when a woman is in a hurry, she still looks for a great relational experience. When she finds a store that she thinks has excellent customer service, she'll return there and tell others about it. She may not spend as much time shopping as she used to, but she wants to be treated with respect.

There is also a good chance that, once a woman becomes convinced that the product she has chosen is the best she can buy, she will promote it widely to others. Whether it's a new health care plan for her business or a pleasant experience buying a fax machine, we know women are brand loyal. In the meantime, sales professionals need to be aware of the relationship building skill that underlies most women's activities, frenzied as they may appear sometimes.

Women enjoy knowing the details about the brand they support, and they can be important allies in the marketing process. If they love it, they'll talk about it. The same goes for a salesperson. If they enjoy the sales interaction, they'll tell their friends or colleagues about you. That's why when you sell well to a woman, you're riding her coattails to possibly dozens of other people. In Chapter 6, we will do an even deeper dive into the importance of relationships in selling to women.

So far, as we have explored selling to women and selling to men, we have examined the genders as separate entities. We know that these situations are typically becoming the minority in selling today. What is more likely the case is that you will be in a sales process involving both genders.

Selling to Women and Men...at the Same Time!

> 90% of American women have veto power over all vehicle and consumer purchases for their own households, and buy 65% of all cars.

For sales people involved in major purchases made by two people, the implications are significant. First, how do you sell to a man and a woman at the same time and make them both feel satisfied? Secondly, if you are selling to businesses, chances are you are dealing with more than one person. For major account sales, you may be selling to a buying committee or decision-making group made up of men and women. It is this combination that, if properly understood, can make you very, very successful.

Couples buy together nowadays, and there are certain products and services that lend themselves to partner purchasing: houses, cars, investment packages, insurance, and major household purchases. This is the time when the adept sales professional has to shift gears between the male and female clients in front of him or her. If a salesman sells almost exclusively to the male partner, he's dead in the water with the woman. When she shoots the sale down by saying that "it's too big," or "it's the wrong size", she's really saying that she never made a connection with the salesman, and may even have felt disrespected. On the other hand, if a saleswoman develops a relationship with the female buyer with lots of details and chatty relationship stuff, the man may check out and the sale is lost. The objection that the man might give, perhaps that "it's too expensive", is merely a cover for his discomfort.

Selling to a male and female at the same time takes skill, and this is where it's even more essential to understand the buying influences of both genders – and that's especially true in business. If you have ever sold to a large account you probably used a mapping process. This is where you map all of the people involved in the sales process and determine their unique reasons for buying your product or service. But as you look at each person and the roles they play, do you treat them differently? My guess is you don't. A buyer is a buyer, isn't it? Well, of course not! So why would you sell to them in exactly the same way? Since this is going to be happening more and more frequently, savvy salespeople will need to change their approach and adjust accordingly.

As we will see in the next few chapters, everything you have been taught about selling will have to change!

In Part II, we'll look at how we've traditionally sold to men and women, and find out that we've basically been doing it wrong for the last 40 years.

TRY THIS ON:

Buy or try out something that you associate with the opposite gender. Evaluate the experience. Put yourself in the sales person's shoes. How would you have sold this product to you?

- Would you have done it differently?
- What did you notice about yourself?

TRY THIS ON:

Look back and review your last sales call in which you were selling to a woman and a man.

- How did their interaction play out in the process?
- Was one person clearly the decision maker?
- How did you prioritize their needs and issues and whose did you choose to address?

LEARNING POINTS FROM THIS CHAPTER

1. Although men are still in charge of most industries, women's numbers in the labor force and in management are increasing and influencing sales.

2. The growth of Women Owned Business and the related purchasing power is staggering.

3. Men tend to be much more transactional in buying style.

4. Women have a buying style that is more relational but may move to transactional based on time and the product.

5. Women tend to be more brand loyal than men, but they'll leave their brand if the service is bad.

6. Selling to men and women at the same time takes skill, flexibility, and an understanding of gender differences.

Part Two

Chapter 4
Understanding the Changing Game of Sales

> The healing power of the Grail is the only thing that can save your father now. It's time to ask yourself what do you **believe?**
> - The mad scientist in *Indiana Jones and the Last Crusade*

As sales professionals, we are constantly searching for the next Holy Grail of sales techniques. What can we say or do differently to be more successful? A quick look at the history of sales and sales training, from the beginning of time until the 1900's, shows us that selling was all about product, location and price. Customers came to you. Then, beginning with the traveling salesman, the product came to the consumer.

The earliest part of the century emphasized order taking, and occasionally wild promotions and promises. In rural areas, salesmen relied on long-term relationships and socializing while selling. By mid-century, with the advent of radio and television advertising, and more competition, learning to be persuasive became popular, along with the Dale Carnegie method of winning friends and influencing people.

> You can make more friends in two months by becoming interested in other people than you can in two years by trying to get other people interested in you.
> -Dale Carnegie

Later, sales methods emphasized the customer-centered approach that downplayed manipulation and looked at the customer's needs instead of the sales person's.

There was no distinction between selling to women or selling to men, of course. It was assumed that sales, the selling process, and the customer were all standard, and that standard was primarily a masculine one. It was created by men for men, and worked very successfully for a very long time.

Sales books focusing on building relationships began to appear. They documented the strengths of relationship building versus the sometimes manipulative approach of transactional selling.

> Over 1,000 books on selling have been written by men.

Relationships were seen as important, but yet almost every book on relational selling ignored the important linkage of gender to the relationship. Only within the last two decades have we seen a distinction made between the communication styles of the two genders, and the creation of sales approaches that are more relational in nature.

Part of the reason for this was that psychological research and writers, including John Gray and Deborah Tannen, had noted that men and women communicate differently. Understanding that the genders communicate differently, marketers started to notice different purchasing habits and began to separate their marketing messages by genders.

> Less than 15 books on selling have been written by women.

The problem was no one told the sales department that these changes were occurring.

Whereas in Part I we explored the changing workplace, gender differences, and sales opportunities, in Part II we focus on the premise that men and women rarely purchase in the same way. Men are largely interested in the transaction, women in the relationship. This simple fact is the founding and most important principle of the book. Now we bring these two seemingly unrelated components together to help you sell.

Simply and clearly stated, there are two very different approaches to selling – the transactional and relational (or relationship) models. These or some variant of them are now used and taught to virtually all sales people. Sales training up to this point has chosen one approach or the other, rarely integrating the two.

Gender differences in the sales world, as in all fields, matter, and we will examine the two most widely used sales models from a gender viewpoint. As you will see, the transactional model, which we discuss in Chapter 5, was written and developed by men, and is dependent on male assumptions and skills.

The transactional model focuses on things men like: facts, data, features, benefits, overcoming objectives, and closing that sale. Powerful things manly things.

> Facts are meaningless. You could use facts to prove anything that's even remotely true!
>
> -Homer Simpson

If we were to do a Gender Traits Test on sales words, these would certainly all fall into the male category! We will use men as our customer for this model.

As we explore relationship selling in Chapter 6, we will use women as our customer. The key words of relational selling are "enthusiasm", "feelings", and "sharing". Are you sensing a pattern here? These are female-associative words.

These are pleasant words, relationship words, and they are exactly what you need to sell in a relational way. As we explore the relational model, we will see that, again, some relational sales books have been written… by men. Men who get it! Men who understand that in order to build long-term sustainable competitive advantage with their customers, you need to build a viable, trust-based relationship.

These are very powerful books designed to earn business for the long run. We just don't often use the word relationship. Perhaps a better term may be bonding, and I can certainly attest to the tens of thousands of dollars I have spent playing golf or hosting big old fashioned steak dinners.

To tell the truth, I was surprised to find in my research that so many of these books had been written by men. Men can build relationships. Great salesmen understand the need to do it.

Noun: Male Bonding
The formation of a close personal relationship with men.
                                        -WordWeb

The need to understand bonding has spawned the release of at least 100 books on relational selling, and while they all talk about the importance of building a relationship, none of these male-authored books examines it from a gender perspective.

Yet to me this seems so obvious. My research has found some books written on the subject by women, who do indeed talk about the gender issue. Women get this intuitively. They have shared their secrets, but, alas, men have not been listening.

In the last chapter of Part Two we will explore how our unique differences play out when we are selling to men and women at the same time. As we have said before, men and women are different; very, very different. In the sales game, we add one more complexity to the situation… money. We want the customer to buy something. I cannot think of a more volatile mix of ingredients than man/woman/money, yet this scenario plays out daily in millions of transactions across the country.

We will explore this concept in two areas. The first is around selling to couples, since many large personal transactions mean selling to couples. This is the blend of relational and transactional selling at its finest and its worst. If you sell houses, cars or financial services -- this is your life! The second area is around selling to business.

Given all of the data you saw in Chapter 1, the workplace is changing. If you sell almost anything of value to a major company, you are dealing with multiple buying influences at the same time -- men and women coming together to buy or lease for their companies. And if you thought the ingredients of gender and money were volatile, just think about adding the fuel of company roles and politics.

Miller-Hieman said, "People don't buy a product per se; they buy what the product will do for them." This means that each person is buying your solution based on his/her own personal win. This is about solving company problems and handling corporate politics, while selling to both genders simultaneously.

If you are reading this book as a seasoned sales professional, you may already have a system or process that you are using. My hope is that it is working for you and you are successful. If you do not have a current process or are not maximizing all of your sales opportunities, then I will show you how I came up with a new, more effective selling process for you to use.

If you currently use a transactional or relational sales process and you are happy with it, you may want to skip Part Two and go straight to the EVOLVE Tool in Part Three. The EVOLVE Tool provides you with ways to overcome your blind spots in the current selling process you use. And while I believe you will be most successful by using the Evolve Selling Process, I know that I may not be able to fundamentally change the way you sell today. As we will see in Part Two, both selling processes have strengths and weaknesses. The EVOLVE Tool is designed to minimize your blind spots regarding selling to different genders -- and even if you decide to stay with your process, you will be more effective in applying EVOLVE to your system

Finally, remember that not all men are transactional. Not all women are relational. In Part Three of our book we will explore a new sales process that addresses the contemporary issue of the increasingly dynamic marketplace.

LEARNING POINTS FROM THIS CHAPTER

1. Most popular sales theories have been the transactional model and the relational sales process.

2. Transactional selling that depends on data, benefits and problem solving has been most comfortable with men and the male way of conducting business.

3. The relational method of selling has been more female in style with its emphasis on the relationship between seller and buyer.

4. A new sales theory is called for, one that takes both the male and the female buying styles into consideration.

Chapter 5
Selling to Men...The Transactional Model

> Women speak because they wish to speak, whereas a man speaks only when driven to speech by something outside himself - like, for instance, he can't find any clean socks.
>
> - Jean Kerr, actress

Over the last 30 years, we have seen the advent of the transactional sales model. Among the many writers on this style of selling, two have stood the test of time: Jack Carew and Neil Rackham, creators of the Diamond and SPIN, respectively.

Developed by Jack Carew and promoted in *You'll Never Get No for an Answer*, transactional selling used a diamond-shaped visual model that included ten strategies for positioning. This technique began to focus on the customer as the cornerstone of the sales process. Still used widely by sales trainers, this model created a selling system that was quite effective in one-on-one selling situations.

Close on the heels of Carew's book appeared a well-researched publication by Neil Rackham that has become another bible of sales. *SPIN Selling* was developed from 35,000 sales calls that gave the author a documented foundation for saying what worked in sales and what didn't.

The gist of the Situation/Problem/Implication/Need-Payoff (SPIN) theory was that asking key questions at important points in the sale process satisfactorily closed the sale.

Overall, transactional selling has worked particularly well with salesmen and male buyers, the norm for its day. To demonstrate this, we'll take a fresh look at a familiar sales situation.

A Tupperware Party – Men's Style!

6:50 PM Buy beer, chips and salsa.
6:55 PM Put chips and salsa in Tupperware bowls.
7:00 PM The Boys arrive.
7:02 PM The Sales Pitch.

Dave: Hey, guys, thanks for coming to my Tupperware party. I wanted to show you their great new collection of bowls. You can put your leftovers in these bowls, freeze them, then take then directly from freezer to microwave and they don't melt.

Steve: Yeah, I hate it when that happens.

Dave: And when I don't have leftovers in them, I use them for serving bowls. Those bowls with the chips and salsa are the new Tupperware bowls.

John: Man, that's great, the less stuff in my cupboards the better.

Dave: The set of 14 bowls in various sizes is $44.99, and if you order tonight you get a free spatula.

Rick: What?! $45 is a lot of money!

Dave: Yeah, but you only have to do dishes once a week, so I always have some clean and some extra in the freezer. And they last forever.

Steve: Cool, I'll take a set.

Rick: Me too, I'll take one.

John: O.K. Count me in.

Dave: I'll have them here next week

Steve and the Guys: Can we watch the game now?

7:08 PM The Tupperware party is over and the guys settle in to watch the game.

Now, I have never attended a Tupperware party and I don't know too many men who have, but I can only imagine that it would be the shortest home sales party on the planet.

I said in the Introduction that most men are largely transactional when they buy. How much is it, and what should I know about the product? Men like facts and figures. And there's nothing wrong with that. It's effective, efficient. Properly used, it may be perfect for the low-ticket, one-time sale. In fact, for many purchases, women want exactly the same thing. And while it may not appear like it, Dave followed a sales process, a very effective sales process. Let's explore the men's Tupperware party from a sales process standpoint.

Transactional selling follows a fairly set series of steps. They may vary a little depending on whose model you look at, but at their core they follow a similar process, which is:

- Open the call and build rapport.
- Discuss why you are there and what you are selling.
- Describe the features, advantages and benefits of your product.
- Prepare to handle objections.
- Close.

Did Dave follow all of these steps? Let's find out.

Analysis of the Men's Tupperware Party

Open the call and build rapport	"Hey guys, thanks for coming to my Tupperware party."
Discuss what you offer	"I wanted to show you their great new collection of bowls."

Describe the features, advantages and benefits of your product	"You can put your leftovers in these bowls, freeze them, then take then directly from freezer to microwave and they don't melt." "And when I don't have leftovers in them, I use them for serving bowls. Those bowls with the chips and salsa are the new Tupperware bowls." "The set of 14 bowls in various sizes is $44.99, and if you order tonight you get a free spatula."
Handle objections	Rick: "$45 is a lot of money!" Dave: "Yeah, but you only have to do dishes once a week, so I always have some clean and some extra in the freezer. And they last forever."
Close	"I'll have them here next week."

We saw price and product in action. What about pleasure? As you recall, "People don't buy a product per se; they buy what the product will do for them." For the men above, the products fill a very functional need. The fact they won't have to do dishes for a while is certainly pleasurable.

You will also notice that our example has a relational component. These guys were Dave's friends and trusted him, or they would not have so quickly agreed to the order. Transactional selling is one way of selling. It's fast and efficient, but improperly used it has many, many blind spots and, quite frankly, without Dave's relationship with his buddies, it would not have worked in the above model. Of interest is how Dave handled objections. While he acknowledged Rick's concern, he really just fired back with an answer. This is how men handle objections, directly, powerfully, with facts. This could be seen as a problem and we'll discuss it later. Under the right conditions, transactional selling can be very effective. Under the wrong circumstances, with the wrong customer, it can be disastrous. It is also the type of sales training that most people have attended or witnessed first hand.

Transactional selling was the first formal sales training I ever received and it helped me to be quite effective, it's also the way that many men buy. By understanding transactional selling, women may be able to be more effective in selling to men. While I do not advocate the transactional process, by understanding it we can see what strengths and weakness are present in the process. Let's break down the transactional model steps.

1. Open the Call and Build Rapport

Individual interpretations of opening the call range from the retail salesperson's "How can I help you?" to an "opening benefit statement." Some transactional sellers aim to build rapport in these early stages. Others downplay the whole process. According to Neil Rackham's SPIN selling technique, "preliminaries… don't play a crucial role in the larger sale." He cautions the salesperson to get down to business quickly, while not talking about solutions too soon, a distracting combination, to say the least. This is transactional selling in its purest form.

There are both positives and negatives to this opening gambit by the transactionalists.

STRENGTHS:
- Building rapport attempts to find common ground, and creates some dialogue.
- This type of opening often suits men well.
- Saleswomen can learn to get to the point quickly, without irritating a male client from the beginning of the transaction, or a female who is looking for a transactional purchase.

WEAKNESSES:

- The rapport mentioned by the theorists is relatively shallow, and sometimes nonexistent.
- Most sales training teaches people to look around the office and relate to things they see. This is not a fact-based technique and it leads to inconclusive data. It also encourages jumping to conclusions.
- The gender bias of most men is to not spend enough time getting to know the customer, and the superficial handling of this topic encourages that. Also, don't forget you may be selling to a relational male.

2. Discuss What You Offer

The next stage is where the salesperson gets down to business and answers the client's unspoken words: Why are you here and what are you selling? This is the opening of the classic sales pitch. Len Serafino, in his transactional book *Sales Talk*, states that the key points at this stage are to develop an organized, well rehearsed presentation, keep it short, and be truthful in answering the client's questions. This basically outlines the transactional approach: give the data and give it well.

STRENGTHS:

- This approach puts on the table what you want your customer to know and do.
- The opportunity for women here is learning to be succinct, to be strong, and to tell the transactional customer why you are there.

WEAKNESSES:

- This is a salesperson-focused technique.
- With the transactional method, the salesperson sometimes tries to sell the customer something they don't need.
- Communication is usually one-way: salesperson to customer.
- The gender bias of most men is to sell their solution and minimize the female customer's need for detail, for the story.

3. Describe the Features, Advantages and Benefits of your Product

This is the most important aspect of the transactional model, and what distinguishes it from previous models. In describing the features of the product, the salesperson is encouraged to enlist the customer's support by asking the right questions and making sure that he empathizes with the customer. As Jack Carew stated, "The key to creating position with the customer is somehow to get out of your OR (Operating Reality, i.e., the salesperson's) and into his (the customer's) OR. And it takes a conscious effort to do that." The emphasis with Neil Rackham is to focus on the information gathering process, enabling the salesperson to highlight how the product fits his/her need. It translates the facts into tangible benefits and minimizes competitive threats.

STRENGTHS:
* This focuses the salesman on the benefits of his product.
* Salesmen tend to sell using facts. These are sometimes features that do not translate to tangible benefits. Effectively used, however, this sequence sells benefits (i.e., what the product will do for the customer).
* The opportunity for women, if selling to men, is to be well armed with facts prior to the sales presentation.

WEAKNESSES:
* Dialogue is usually a one-way street.
* Men often sell with facts that are of little interest to women.
* A gender tendency of salesmen is to not value the questions that women raise, or the answers women give to the salesman's questions.
* Yet another tendency is to talk down to women.

4. Handle Objections

This is the stage at which the salesperson handles customer issues related to the product solutions. It may be used at any time during the sales process. Vital to this phase in Carew's Diamond is his Response Check, which allows the sales pro to handle any problems that the customer has as they come up. With constant enquiry and feedback about the customer's deliberations, "The Response Check gives the customer a chance to get involved. You don't end up moving into a Closure when he's stalled somewhere back at the beginning with a nagging concern about something you mentioned during the Solution step." Asking questions, again, becomes important at this point.

STRENGTHS:

- This step helps the salesperson to prioritize the issues apparent to the customer and handle them one at a time.
- It minimizes competitive threats.
- Done properly, objections may be a way of getting or giving more information to allow the customer to make a decision.
- It uses a sequential process to slow down the salesmen's process and not jump to conclusions.
- The opportunity for women, if selling to men, is that they may be forced to deal with win/lose situations, rather than a win/win. Staying focused and being direct with facts is the challenge to women here.

WEAKNESSES:

- Most books on selling encourage the salesman to bully their way through the process.
- Most salesmen pick a few key points that only reinforce their solution and restate it to the customer.
- The tendency of some men is to be condescending and not respect the question that a female customer raises.
- Another tendency for men is to not listen effectively, or to have selective listening when objections are raised.

5. Close

This is the point of confirmation by both parties that the sale has been made. The salesperson restates his/her solution to the customer, so that they feel good about the decision. Transactional writers urge a relatively low-key approach to the close, ("I'll have them here next week.").

According to Len Sarafino, the five key strategies for closing the sale are the following:

- Look for buying signs that suggest the customer is ready to close.
- Keep it simple and direct.
- Don't be afraid to ask more than once.
- Be confident, not cocky.
- When you've made the sale, shut up.

STRENGTHS:
- The close signals completion of the deal so everyone knows where they stand.
- Once the sales person knows how to close and can read the buying signals, it may speed the process along.
- The gender opportunity for women is to not over sell or over communicate, to close when the client is ready.

WEAKNESSES:
- Too many books (and sales people) focus on manipulative forms of closure.
- The tendency of men is to attempt to close too quickly before all issues have been addressed.
- Sometimes salesmen don't understand that when a woman says, No, she means NO.
- Women sometimes see salesmen as being manipulative in their haste to close.

Some Final Thoughts on Transactional Selling

We have described transactional selling as an essentially male model, created by men for selling to men. This is not to say that this model is useless, because it has been used successfully for the last couple of decades. But remember, selling, particularly in this country, is like trying to hit a moving target.

Customers never stay in one place. The latest news out of the retail industry is that younger men don't shop like older men. They learn to shop earlier, spend more time in the malls, and are closer in buying styles to younger women than the Boomer men. In other words, things change, even the style with which men buy. The tools and techniques that we are going to give you fit this shifting terrain. So, if you think that you would like to expand your market, keep up with gender dynamics, and sharpen your sales skills for the new market you are sure to encounter, the EVOLVE Tool might be your answer.

Transactional selling provides great learning techniques for women who want to understand what works in a man's world. Being concise, sticking to the facts, listening carefully to objections, and aiming for precise answers can be challenges for women entering the sales arena for the first time. The discipline involved assists in making the shift into a man's head and making the sale in a way with which he's comfortable.

However, men, beware! There are big pitfalls for men who have only learned and only use the transactional method when it comes to selling to women. Transactional selling is not going to work with most females, ever! In fact, it turns them off. Issues like limiting the relationship-building stage and closing quickly can become obstacles to selling to women, who often want to establish trust at the beginning and be allowed to make up their minds slowly at the end. A woman may often double back and ask the same question twice, merely seeking validation. The impatient salesman who doesn't understand how a woman's mind works ends up losing far more sales than they could ever make.

In response to this problem, several writers and lecturers have emerged to discuss that previously nebulous area of selling to women. As they've all pointed out, it's a whole different ballgame.

LEARNING POINTS FROM THIS CHAPTER

1. The steps in the transactional model follow the way men think – and handle a sale. These are: open the call, discuss what you offer, describe the features and benefits, handle objections, and close the sale.

2. Learning the transactional model can be helpful for women selling to men.

3. The weaknesses of this model are as follows: relationship building is downplayed, communication tends to be one way, the female buyer's need for detail and connection are often ignored, and the closure of the sale can become manipulative.

4. The challenge for the saleswoman in selling to a man is to stay focused, be direct with facts, and not over-communicate.

Selling to Men Selling to Women

Chapter 6
Selling to Women...The Relational Theory

A major stockbroker told me he has oriented his practice toward female clients – with great success. A research nut, he reports that his average male client recommends him to 2.6 others. On the other hand, his women clients recommend him to an average of 21 other people. **Yes, that's two-point-six versus twenty-one.**

- Tom Peters from *Re-Imagine!*

I learned this lesson very early on in my sales career. When I graduated from college, the unemployment rate was close to 20 percent. There were no jobs to be found. I ended up taking a job selling beauty supplies on full-scale commission. If you didn't sell anything, you didn't get paid. Now I have to tell you that most shampoos, conditioners, hair color and permanent waves are pretty much the same, and most salons have between six and eight different reps calling on them. Pricing, products and delivery were all basically the same.

This was my first exposure to relationship selling. The salesperson who got to know the salon owner, spent time understanding her (occasionally his) business, and, quite frankly, spent a lot of time listening would wind-up with all the sales. All the salon owners knew each other, and they referred the best sales people to their friends. In two years of building relationships, I moved my territory from the fourth largest in the district to the largest territory in the country, and in the process won a new car.

Since the products we were all selling were very similar, and there are about 200 new hair care products introduced every year, my personal selling skills made all the difference. When I had a new product introduction, the salon owner would try it because of our relationship.

Trust me, beauty salons really do not need one more product line to sell. However the salon owner knew that I would help her make more money because I listened, invested time, and really chose to understand her and her business. While trust is important in any relationship, at this stage of my career I did not understand the importance of applying this in a more formal manner. What I learned was that as much as your customers may trust you, without a formal process you will leave the door open for competitors to come in and develop a better relationship with your customer.

As we said in our chapter on *Selling to Men*, these are not absolute statements, but relationships are critically important in selling to women. I actually believe that sustaining great relationships with your customers is in fact genderless. It is also the type of sustainable advantage that drives long-range arrangements with customers, but given the propensity for relationships we will use women as our primary customers for this chapter. We will begin by exploring why relationships are so important to women. This links to our physiological and psychological reasons discussed in Chapter 2. We will explore the psychology of relationships and relationship selling and see that it's something that all customers want out of the sales experience. We will see that men are relational; it just looks a lot different from our female model. We will look at a framework for relationship selling and examine the strengths and weaknesses that may be present, given the gender bias involved in the selling process.

Where it All Starts

So much has been written and spoken and taught about the physiological and psychological differences between men and women that it seems redundant to do it all again. However, for those readers who skipped Chapter 2, let me just sum up the major points and add a few new ones.

Women's brains have prepared them to have stronger emotional responses to events than men, and to remember those events. Her brain structure from infancy also makes her more language competent than her male counterpart, and three times more communicative. A woman's hormones and social influences also compel her to bond with others when she's under stress.

This makes your female customer different from you, fellows, in at least a few ways that impact the sales process:

- She is an emotional being.
- She focuses on relationships.
- She has a wide-angle view of the proceedings.
- She enjoys the process as well as the result.
- She gets faster intuitive messages about people and events.
- She gathers more detailed information.
- She likes to help others.
- She is a joiner.

Retailers are now creating a profile of the typical female consumer. Valerie Otto, a gender consumer specialist, lists the five basic factors to bear in mind when selling to women. Says Otto:

- A woman buys with both her head and her heart.
- Women respond to convenience.
- Women can see through any standard sales pitch.
- Women often buy from the periphery.
- Women care about whom they buy from.

With the strengthening of women's presence in the workplace, and the buying power they now have, we ignore the new sales research at our peril.

The Evolution of the Relationship Theory

All of the indicators point in one direction for sales: more targeted selling, and the need for a relational model that will better prepare the entire sales force to reach a busier, more informed, more selective, and more female audience. Let me start by saying I am certainly not the first person to come up with the idea that selling to women is different than selling to men. My model is a new development, but it has many forebears who have experimented with various selling techniques and theories about relationship formation.

The relationship, or relational theory of selling has developed over the last 20 years. One of the earliest writers on the subject was the incredible Mary Kay, a woman some might say with a whole lot of testosterone, who in 1981 wrote one of the first modern testimonials to relationship selling. This was empathy at its best. Mary Kay explored the sales process from the client's needs first, rather than from the sales person's, and she made millions doing it.

In later years, the social sciences were to add more depth and material to the field of selling. Going beyond the straight transaction, moving away from the hard data and into the psychology of successful selling had become a major concern of many theorists, some of them men. Robert Miller and Stephen Heiman's *Conceptual Selling* came out of the psycho-social sciences with its emphasis on communication at every juncture of the sale. The theory they created was influenced by their Superb Communication Process (or SCP).

> Our entire philosophy at Mary Kay is based on the golden rule – we sometimes call it the Go-Give principle. We focus on **giving** instead of **getting.** We use the Go-Give principle, for instance, in training our Beauty Consultants.
>
> We constantly stress that a Consultant should never have dollar signs in her eyes, thinking, "How much can I sell these people today?" Instead, think in terms of "What can I do so these women will leave here today feeling better about themselves".
>
> - Mary Kay Ash
> *Mary Kay: The Success Story of America's Most Dynamic Businesswoman*

SCP = Getting Information + Giving Information + Getting Commitment. It was a customer-driven rather than a salesman-driven process. In my mind this had been one of the missing pieces. It was a great process that used a looser structure to drive long-term customer commitment. In 1992 Miller and Heiman also published the *Large Account Management Process - LAMP*, which motivated the salesperson to continually upgrade the relationship with the customer, until the latter sees the salesperson as an ally, paid by someone else.

> You don't sell a product or a service; you sell a relationship. In this relationship, prospects buy you as an authority in your field – a person who can be trusted to do the best possible job for them.
>
> Orv Owens
> *The Psychology of Relationship Selling*

Orv Owens moved into the field of personal development, sales style, in *The Psychology of Relationship Selling.* He pioneered the approach of the sales person beginning the sales process internally. As Owens saw it, the sales professional needed to work internally on self-esteem and self-image before developing a positive relationship with a client.

In a blend of New Age and positivist terminology, Owens wrote that, whereas a "clerk" sells cost = value, a professional sales person creates value by first becoming the best possible person and then developing a dynamic relationship with the buyer that adds "dimension upon dimension of high-level beliefs or positive decisions."

The 1990s also saw a small handful of female sales theorists who were ready to voice their own ideas about how female clients buy. *Gender Sell: How to Sell to the Opposite Sex*, by Judith C. Tingley and Lee E. Robert, described how salespeople could build relationships with female customers. The tools included communication skills that women typically use when forming relationships with each other. Tingley and Robert based their recommendations on the findings of their own Sales Preference Survey of 600+ participants. As good as this and other books written about selling to women were considered, they had one problem. None of the female authors were sales people; they were communications experts.

In addition to communication specialists, some marketing futurists began to discuss the topic. Faith Popcorn's book on the strategic development of building a relationship with the female customer, *Eveolution: The Eight Truths of Marketing to Women,* has now become a reference book on the subject. Popcorn uses an approach that is "a systemic redefinition that leads to dozens and dozens of subtle shifts and fine alterations." She sees women as not only a major buying force, but as a completely different sort of entity.

As far as Popcorn is concerned, women are joiners, and make a much better long-term market because of it. They join brands, just as they do gardening clubs and political parties, and they become loyal customers. She highlights companies that have climbed onto the bandwagon, from Saturn to Tiffany and Nike. Companies that have researched women's needs and interests and found ways to appeal to them, and she encourages firms to create ways in which women can connect with other women.

> A customer of the moment is the one who buys your brand; a customer for life is the one who joins it.
>
> Faith Popcorn
> *Eveolution*

Another woman who has had an influence on sales attitudes is Dr. Pat Heim, author of *Hardball for Women*. Heim points out that even in athletic coaching of professional athletes, how coaches handle males and females is completely different. Male athletes respond well to strength and intimidation. Female athletes, on the other hand, want connection and a response to their humanity. Even women we think have the most testosterone, it seems, want a relationship with their coaches.

Mapping the Relationship Theory

Relationship selling has traits of the female, with all of its empathy and connecting principles. Some people even think it should be limited to selling to women. What we sometimes forget is that men are relational too; it just looks a lot different from the bonding experience of women. Everyone will agree that men occasionally have a need to gather together with other men, whether to play golf or to go to bars or sporting events. They may not communicate with each other in the same way as women, but they certainly connect. They may be competitive rather than consensus building, but they relish the competition with others.

Hormones have a significant impact on how we relate to each other. Research now tells us that when a man's testosterone is down he feels depressed, and he drives it up by doing something physical or competitive (even if it's watching a sporting event). When a woman's oxytocin is down, she feels better by getting together with others, by chatting with a friend, or by crying and getting it off her chest. The hunter's way of bonding is different from the gatherer's, but one need we all have is to be liked and respected by others: it is universal. It's just how we go about it.

In order to map the relational process, I thought that going back to the Tupperware party would be a good way to show the difference between the transactional and relational processes. The guys at the Tupperware party were focused on the bottom-line, quick to talk over objections, ready to get the whole process over with... and then bond over beer and a game. Let's look at a whole other way of operating – the women's version. It demonstrates the major differences between the typical male and female ways of buying and selling, and forms a great argument for using different selling styles.

While I could write pages on the range of topics that might be discussed in a couple of hours of a women's Tupperware party, I have decided to merely capture some of the key topics that might come up at the party.

Introduction to new Tupperware collection, welcome to late arrivals, compliments about outfits and lost weight, recipe for appetizers made in new Tupperware, parents' vacation to Hawaii, daughter's softball game, boss being a jerk at work, $44.99, free spatula, freezer safe, search for a new dentist, upcoming mammogram, multiple color options, what Oprah's reading, hosting bunko next week, dishwasher safe, dealing with a sick pet, finding a housekeeper you can trust, I can have it for you next week.

The lone, frustrated man who happens to be listening in on this Tupperware party, if he can overcome his discomfort with the proceedings, will notice that the communication has a fluid nature. It's not anywhere as formal as the transactional process. He might even ask, Is there any process at all?

Well, the answer is yes. Relational selling has a process, but it may not fall into a linear model. Let's explore some linkages to our transactional model.

Welcome to late arrivals, compliments about outfits and weight lost, *recipe for appetizers made with new Tupperware,* Introduction to new Tupperware collection, parents' vacation to Hawaii, daughter's softball game, boss being a jerk at work, *$44.99, free spatula, freezer safe,* search for a new dentist, upcoming mammogram, *multiple color options,* what Oprah's reading, hosting bunko next week, *dishwasher safe,* dealing with a sick pet, finding a housekeeper you can trust, **I can have it for you next week.**

Open the Call and Build Rapport
Discuss What You Offer
Describe the Features, Advantages and Benefits of your Product
Handle Objections/Issues
Close/Deliver Customer Satisfaction
These are coded to see how the steps of a transactional model may show themselves in a relational situation

Although it's difficult to connect to a linear model like the male transactional model, it does flow through all of the stages in the transactional process.

- Planning is a key component. Making the food ahead of time from the recipe, shopping, inviting people over are critical to success.
- There's a lot of time spent building rapport in fact, much more time than with the transactional process. Although it's almost hidden in the relationship building, the customers' needs are identified (family, time, health, convenience).
- Value is created by pointing out the benefits.
- There's no need to handle objections because the sales person understands the customer so well. However, it is important for the relationship to discuss any issues that may be present but not out in the open.
- The close is natural, almost assumed (i.e., deliver customer satisfaction now and in the future).

While we may have oversimplified what goes on at a women's Tupperware party, I did this to illustrate a point. If you examine the physiological and psychological nature of relationships, it's easy to conclude that they are in fact present in many business situations. We may just not see or acknowledge them.

Selling to women in business is obviously tougher than the visual depicted in the Tupperware party. However, if relationships are important to women, and you are selling to them in a business setting, you better be more flexible, more open and better prepared to exchange information.

The Relational Theory - Strengths and Weaknesses

The problem with the Relational Model is that there isn't one, (a visual model). As hard as we looked, we couldn't find any systematic model that dissected and mapped relationship selling. This isn't unusual, of course, given the fact that women often don't think in spatial, model-like terms. But even the relational theories and techniques described by male writers don't include a model or visualization.

Working in diversity education and as a sales trainer, I understand at a deep level that selling to women takes special skills and training. As we've discussed repeatedly, women are different from men, and in many circumstances they purchase differently as a result of their differences. I believe that relational selling has a definite role to play in contemporary selling, just as there continues to be a need for transactional selling.

However, as a man, and a 20-year salesman, I have a problem with the vagueness around most of the relationship theories, in comparison to the transactional models. Most of the literature and training around relationship selling confirms the need to establish meaningful relationships, and to add value to the sale by listening, asking the right questions, and empathizing with the client.

The weakness of this argument, however, is that there are times when neither a man nor a woman wants a relationship with the sales person. They may have already done their research, know exactly what they want, or be in a hurry to purchase. The relational theories tend to be strong on the connection side, but weaker on the side of the transactional buyer, whether male or female.

In order to avoid this problem, and to make the relationship process more structured, I have created a meaningful tool and model that fit my linear mind. In this way, I've used the functions of the transactional model and applied what we know about the different traits and behaviors of each gender to create a brand new relational model that works for selling to either a man or a woman. The Evolved Selling Model is described in detail in Chapter 10 and it is the linear model of relational selling.

Additionally, to strengthen the model, I will introduce a powerful tool that allows the seller flexibility during the sales process. So flexible is the tool that it allows the sales person to use it during that most difficult of sales – selling to couples! So before we get into this new process, let's explode one more gender dynamic, the dynamic of selling to a man and a woman at the same time.

LEARNING POINTS FROM THIS CHAPTER

1. Women are biologically more emotional than men, and they buy more emotionally.

2. Women tend to trust people with whom they can form a relationship.

3. A woman's buying style (relational) differs from the typical male style (transactional) in that there is more and deeper communication between buyer and seller during the entire sales process.

4. When a woman likes a product or a salesperson, she lets others know, lots of others.

Chapter 7
Selling to Women and Men…at the Same Time!

> **Chandler:** Okay, well. Janice said 'Hi, do I look fat today?' And I, I looked at her....
> **Ross:** Whoa, whoa, whoa. You looked at her? You never look. You just answer; it's just a reflex. Do I look fat? Nooo! Is she prettier than I am? Noo! Does size matter?
> **Rachel:** Noooooooo!
> — *Friends,* television series

One of my goals in writing this book was to present a well researched book on selling, and to get into the heads of men and women at the same time. I have presented data on the business case for understanding gender differences. I found mounds of research on actual gender differences and communication style. I found hundreds of books on selling. And through all my research, I found exactly two chapters, yes, two chapters written on the subject of selling to women and men at the same time.

Two chapters? Based on all of the research I have seen on buying patterns, gender differences and the marketplace, there should be a boxed encyclopedia set on this subject. And while I am only adding one chapter on the subject, I will give you a few new tools to be successful in these situations. In this chapter, I will set the context and then we will later explore applying the tools in this unique situation.

So far we have explored binary selling, selling to men or selling to women. Now we will explore selling to men and women at the same time on two fronts, first in non-business settings and secondly in the business world.

Selling to Men and Women in Non-Business Settings

I have a friend who is a successful salesman of life insurance and financial services. Greg spends his life sitting in people's homes selling across the kitchen table. When I told him about the idea for the book, he chuckled and immediately got it. "It's funny; we don't talk about it in the industry, but we do sell much differently to women than to men." He shared the following story.

He was selling term life insurance to a young couple who had three small children. The wife had arranged for Greg to come over. From the very start, it was obvious the husband did not want to be involved in this. Through his laptop, Greg laid out financial scenarios on the husband passing or the wife passing. Given that the children were young and she was a stay-at-home mom, Greg estimated that they would need between $500,000 and $1,000,000 in coverage on the husband and between $250,000 and $500,000 on the wife. Greg laid out the need for funds for college, day care and all of the important expenses that lay in front of them if one of them should pass. And at their age, they could get all of this coverage for under $150 a month. It was obvious that Greg was connecting with the young mother and really supporting her concerns. When Greg asked the question, "Well, what do you think?", he was floored when the husband looked at his wife and said, "If you think I'm going to leave you a million dollars to spend when I'm gone, you're crazy!"

Now Greg had heard stories like this but he had never really been involved in one. This guy's mental model was that, if he wasn't around, she'd be out partying on the million dollars, not staying at home raising her children. As she was holding back tears, she thanked Greg for his time and said they would be in touch. Well, as Greg recounted the meeting it was quite obvious that he had not really adequately explored the needs of the husband. This is quite common in selling life insurance. Men think they are invincible, but will usually buy some coverage for their wives, since they realize that there are significant expenses associated with raising children without a spouse. They identify with the male problem, not the female. The female looks at it from both sides.

The story does have a happy ending though. About two days later, Greg got a call from the wife asking for $250,000 worth of coverage on her and $500,000 on her husband. As he thanked her, he could only think about the amount of grief the husband must have endured for his comment that night in the kitchen. He made the fatal mistake; he actually said out loud what he was thinking. He was insensitive, uncaring and in Greg's opinion only heard a few key words:

- I'm dead.
- She gets $1,000,000.
- It costs me almost $200 a month, and I'm not even dead yet.

Is this surprising? Well, if we think back to our chapter on gender differences, the husband had heard only the hard data. Remember, men like facts. One of the keys to selling insurance is to paint a picture of a lifetime of security for your family and loved ones. Unfortunately, the very thought of this doesn't fit with men. What Greg learned is that you must also be sensitive to the facts surrounding "a lifetime of security."

He now spends time talking about day care costs, household upkeep, and the other tangible expenses that happen when one of the spouses dies. As difficult as this is to hear sometimes, these are the facts that many men need to hear... and understand.

Now, selling to couples is not as easy as selling facts to him and developing a relationship with her. Success in selling to couples is applying relational selling and transactional selling at the same time, and that's what makes it so hard. No current sales technology has done this... until now.

Selling to Men and Women in Business at the Same Time

For the researcher and the sales professional, simultaneous dual-gender selling in business settings is truly uncharted waters. As little as has been written on the subject, in today's business environment this may be the most challenging of all sales, and I have discovered this personally.

In my last ten years in selling, I was dealing with large account selling. I sold multi-million dollar cooperative marketing agreements to many of the largest retailers in the country. These programs would be sold to a committee of merchandising, operations, finance, marketing and information technology managers. In doing this selling, we became very successful by mapping all of the people involved in the process. We would identify the roles we believed they played in the process. We would identify who we thought would be problems or supporters of our program. We even identified the administrative assistants of the committee members so that we could ensure our access to the committee members if we needed it.

We made one fatal mistake. We totally ignored the gender of each committee member and how we might have needed to communicate (i.e., sell) differently to these people. For example, we might have needed to invest significantly more time developing a relationship with the female Vice President of Merchandising than we do with the Male Vice President of IT.

Most books on selling, even in large account selling, treat these people as the same. Most books would acknowledge that the VP of merchandising is evaluating your proposal differently than the VP from IT. These books would say that you will only be successful if your product satisfies all their needs. We know that they are approving your solutions for different reasons, (i.e., merchandising needs a 'wow' factor for its consumers, and IT needs to know that your ordering and delivery platform matches their company's infrastructure).

What we usually don't take into account is that we may need to spend more time investing in a relationship with her or being brief and selling only facts to him. My guess is that you, my reader sales person, haven't spent that time. In addition to the challenges of multiple buyers, you also have to take into account that she may not want a relationship (but wants facts and data) and the IT VP needs to understand a lot more about you (and your company, the value of your products and services, and how you will support him well after the sale).

If this all sounds very confusing… it is! On top of all these unique gender dynamics is the interdependency of corporate roles. I know hundreds of women in business who behave completely differently on the job from how they are outside of the workplace.

I have a great friend who is the sales manager for a beverage distributor. She is the only female in management at this company and manages a group of over 150 male truck drivers, merchandisers and sales men. At work she is as tough as she needs to be. Away from work, however, she gardens and describes herself as "a girly girl". When I asked her about this double life, she said it's very hard, but it's what she needs to do.

This is what makes selling so challenging. To assume all women want relationships and all men want facts would be the wrong conclusion to make. The critical factor is being aware of the differences, observing the signals, and being prepared to shift gears at a moment's notice. Planning, seeking facts, valuing each buyer individually and uniquely are the foundations of this book -- and the selling model that we will explore in the next few chapters.

LEARNING POINTS FROM THIS CHAPTER

1. Developed over the last 20 years, the relational model emphasizes establishing a positive relationship with the buyer, male or female.

2. Women often buy in an indirect way that includes relationship building in the process even as they cover all of the steps of the Transactional Model.

3. Relational theories are often vague and difficult for male sales professionals to follow.

4. There are times when neither a man nor a woman wants a relationship with the salesperson.

5. When selling to men and women together, plan a strategy prior to the call to deal the unique dynamics of the situation.

Part Three

Chapter 8
The Evolved Selling Model

> In my house I'm the boss. My wife is just the decision maker.
>
> - Woody Allen

In Chapter 6, Selling to Women…The Relational Theory, I talked about relational selling and how critically important it is to sell to women -- to all customers -- in a relational way. I began to explore relational selling and how it relates to transactional selling. While being a huge advocate for the need to build long-range relationships to be successful with customers, I pointed out that I thought the theory had a couple of weaknesses for me personally.

The first weakness I saw was that it really lacked a structure for my linear male mind to understand. I need a picture, a model, and something firm, not squishy. Secondly, though I know relationships are important, most salespeople have been trained in transactional selling. How then do the two link and how can I evolve myself from a transactional salesman to a relational salesperson? With these two objectives in mind, I decided to map what a relational selling model might look like.

The first thing I found is that it is difficult to connect a holistic (female) model to a linear (male) model, because one flows back and forth, and the other progresses systematically from one stage to another. However, to help us think sequentially we will use the framework for the female Tupperware party. We captured the conversation in a circle. This is not merely conversation however; it is relationship building. The process is going on to move the sale forward, but it is not a linear process that goes from step one to step five like the transactional process. The relational selling model flows back and forth, reconnecting on data and building the relationship.

An illustration of the sales process taking place at the party may look like this:

Visual of a Relational Model

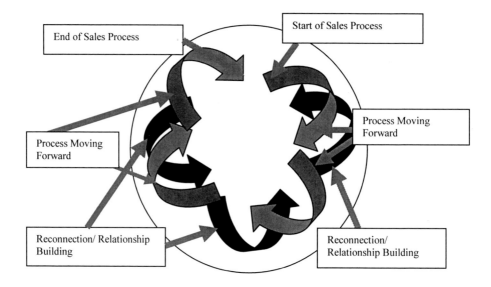

The sales process, as well as the relationship building, is depicted as moving forward and backward. What they are really doing is evolving. I have illustrated the relationship process as arrows moving backward to reconnect. It is not a backward motion but validation. In relations there is a need to constantly revalidate where we are and how we are connecting with the other party. This revalidation is ongoing and it lets you continue to deepen your position with other people and other customers.

If we look at the reconnection process over a series of sales, it might look like this:

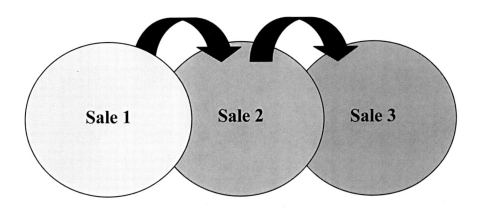

Deepening your relationship will allow you to validate your position on every sales call. If selling can be put into a model, then let's build on our circle and examine key pieces.

Going forward we will use the circle as a model of relational selling. Using a circle as our model, we will examine six critical steps that take place in relational selling. The steps of our relational model are as follows:

- Plan for Success
- Establish the Relationship
- Identify Customer's Needs
- Create Value with your Solution
- Resolve Issues
- Deliver Customer Satisfaction

The following is a quick overview of each step and how it ties to the transactional model. In Chapter 10, we will explore each step in greater detail and see how a new sales model has evolved.

Step 1: Plan for Success

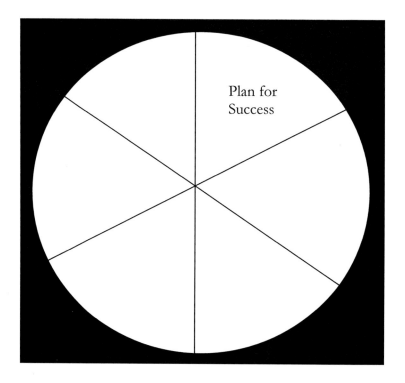

Planning is the most overlooked tool in a salesperson's arsenal. Spending time getting to understand your product line is critically important, but really knowing your customers and why they buy will allow you to have a solid relationship with them.

One key in the planning phase is to think about how to apply our knowledge of gender differences and communication systems and to truly understand their unique concerns, challenges or problems. In relationship selling, the salesperson is able to develop a deeper understanding of the human behind the buyer not just the role they play. By understanding that gender does play a role in understanding the person, the salesperson will better be able to develop a long, healthy relationship with the customer.

Many sales books describe the necessary steps to prepare for a sales call.

Some of these are:

- Use positive self talk to motivate.
- Have complete familiarity with the product.
- Practice the presentation.
- Research the buyer's need.
- Complete a competitive assessment or SWOT (strengths, weaknesses, opportunities and threats) analysis.

In Chapter 9 we will ask you to add one component for your planning purposes, and that is explore the gender of the buyer and plan accordingly. This is the introspective part of planning, and the most difficult. However, with practice, it becomes automatic, particularly when the positive results start to come back.

When selling to another gender, it becomes essential for the salesperson to ask:

- What possible blind spots do I have?
- How will I plan to overcome them?

Later we will discuss a mental model called the EVOLVE Tool that will help you in your planning. For now, just notice what you notice. If you believe any gender issues may be present, it is here in the planning phase that you will begin to address them.

Step 2: Establish the Relationship

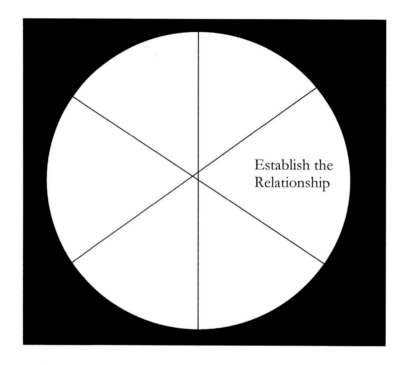

In the transactional model, this is often the most under-utilized step. A significant amount of time needs to be spent building rapport, or establishing and strengthening the relationship. Unfortunately, most sales processes ignore or gloss over this critical step. Some sales books even call this 'chit-chat'. By not valuing this step, the sales professional is not valuing the buyer. Spending time getting to know the person, and their needs and wants, as defined by them, is the most critical step in relationship selling. It's not just about becoming familiar with personal issues, but about knowing the needs and wants relevant to your product that create value for the salesperson and result in time well spent in building a trusting sales relationship.

Building true rapport is also the most challenging step. It is important to walk the fine line between the business and personal relationship. In our female Tupperware example, the sale is made because the relationship is primarily personal. However, building relationships in business is so much more. It's about genuinely connecting the customer with your product. We therefore need to value both the role the customer play's in the sales process, and the person.

In many sales situations, it is very challenging to develop a relationship in just a few minutes. However, the principles remain the same. Don't pre-judge or make assumptions, just seek facts. In business, you may be selling to the same customer over and over again. In those cases you may get to know the customer on a more personal level.

Step 3: Identify the Customer's Needs

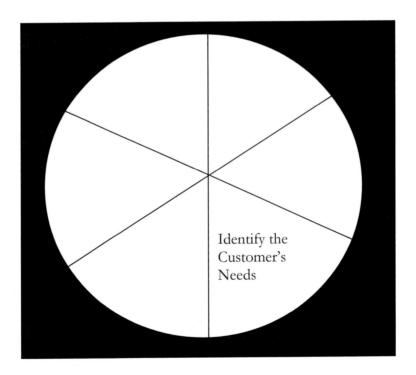

Relational selling is probably an oxymoron. In true relational selling, you are not selling at all. Done properly, you have identified exactly what the customer wants, and you merely supply the solution. This can only be done by genuinely understanding what the customer needs and wants. Identifying needs and wants is not selling; it's about gathering data, which is all about questioning. Questioning, genuinely listening and truly valuing the information you are presented with will support a great relationship.

For the second and third steps of our model, you should be doing less than half of the talking. And that talking should involve the gathering of data and the validation of the information. These both link to the planning phase. What questions are you prepared to ask to get more information? What facts do you need to validate? Only once you have listened, valued, and validated can you begin to share your solution.

Step 4: Create Value with Your Solution

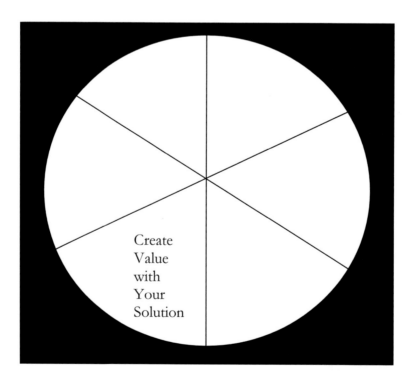

Once you have truly identified the customer's needs, you can start telling your story. If you truly understand the customer's needs and wants, you can begin to apply your unique product attribute to their problem. This is not selling; this is bringing them a solution to their problem. Only now should you begin to convey product information, and then only the information that they need for their solution.

This is often where a salesperson has the tendency to oversell or tell the customer everything they think the buyer needs to know. If you realized during your planning phase that you are the overly conversational type, you should be particularly cautious not to oversell your product. If you truly understand your customer's needs, then you can provide just enough information for them to feel comfortable with your solution. If you have truly met your customer's needs, you can write up the sale and discuss payment terms. There is no hard closing needed if the job has been done properly.

Step 5: Resolve Issues

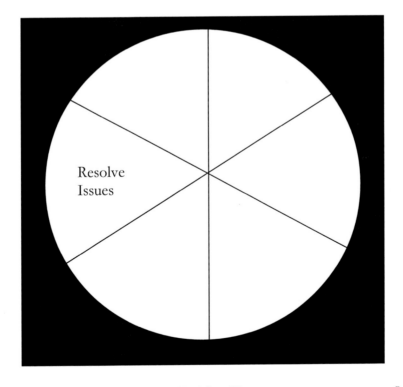

In transactional selling, this is when most salespeople would "handle objectives" or merely dismiss the buyer's needs as irrelevant, (think of Dave in the men's Tupperware party). In the Evolved Selling Model, issues are a topic we want to get onto the table to be able to discuss openly.

In sales, as in all relationships, problems sometimes come up. They can be prior issues, competitive pressures, or any one of a host of unforeseen problems. And while you have hopefully uncovered these in the Identifying Customer's Needs area, now is the time to discuss issues so that you can more readily deliver on the customer needs and make them feel valued in the process.

If you truly understand your customer's needs and how your solutions uniquely satisfy them, then any remaining issues should be minimal. But if issues arise, one of a few things is happening. It could be that the customer may not have truly understood his or her own needs, the needs may have changed since you talked last, or a new competitor may have come into the picture. While this information may have come out during your information gathering stage, the possibility exists that it hasn't.

At this point in a solid relationship, the salesperson must validate that the customer is in fact comfortable, that they are satisfied with the decision and feel good about it. This is the foundation of a relationship. A great challenge for a salesperson is often restating to the customer what the customer has committed to do. Many salespeople think that this may undo the sale or think the customer is getting cold feet.

Chances are there is something you have not uncovered and whether you like it or not, if you don't put it on the table, it will come up later and undo the sale. Even if the customer does not say anything to you, they will certainly not be comfortable in referring you to another customer. Restating what the customer has committed to and having them agree to it, therefore, allows you to close the order, without ever asking for it.

Step 6: Deliver Customer Satisfaction

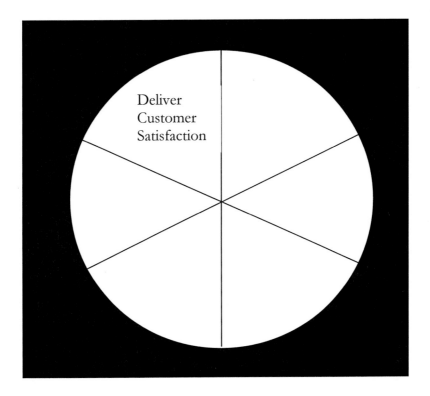

This is now the easy part. If you have planned your work, invested in a relationship, understood your customer's needs, and satisfied them with your unique solution, then the final thing to do is honor your commitments. This will build a foundation for sustainable business now and in the future. You won't just get referrals for three other customers but many more, if you deliver what you promised. You will be delivering solutions that fill real needs to customers who want your solutions.

This is sales after the service, an often neglected part of the sale but a critical step in relational selling. It connects the first sale with future sales and supports the relational linkage of women. This is the most critical step in keeping relationships live.

A New Sales Model Evolves

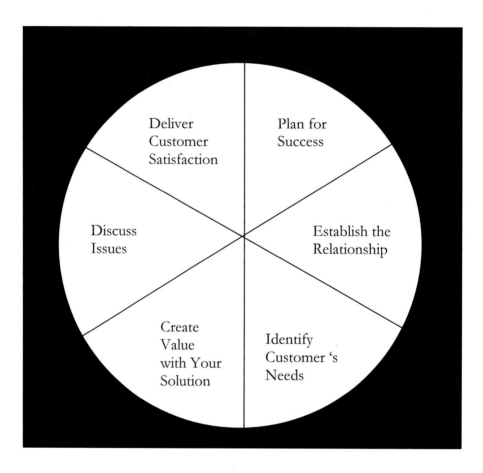

As you have seen, the Evolved Sales Model is a linear process that will feel familiar to most salespeople using the transactional selling model. We have applied relational selling to a circular and linear process in order to create a more flexible and responsive process. This places customer needs and values in the proper perspective, and we have identified key work the salesperson must do in each step. We will explore each step further in Chapter 10 along with ways in which men and women differ in relation to the steps.

This model evolved out of extensive research into sales and sales processes, research into gender differences, and a study of what is going on during each step of the sales process. The Tupperware example is easy to recall and it will allow you, in the moment, to recall both gender differences and the Evolved Selling Process. Selling, real selling, is much harder than depicted, but the principles I have laid out are the same.

Most women who read about the Tupperware parties will laugh at the men's part and be a bit annoyed at the women's version. I have attempted to poke a little fun at both genders, and obviously I am not trying to say that women in business behave like women at a Tupperware party. They can be just as tough and as challenging as any man in any situation. But whether you are selling to a man or a woman in today's environment, a relational approach is the only way you will gain long-term competitive advantage and keep all of your customers happy.

LEARNINGS FROM THIS CHAPTER

1. A new sales model, the Evolved Selling Model, was developed from the latest research about gender differences and takes both genders' needs into consideration.

2. The Evolved Model takes the sales professional through six steps: Plan for Success, Establish the Relationship, Identify Customer's Needs, Create Value with Your Solution, Discuss Issues, and Deliver Customer Satisfaction.

3. While working the Evolved Sales Model, it's important for the seller not to make assumptions about the client while being familiar with likely gender differences and examining his or her own judgments and behavior.

Selling to Men Selling to Women

Chapter 9
The EVOLVE Tool

> My girlfriend says I never listen to her. At least I think that's what she says.
>
> - Seen on a T-shirt

Up to this point, *Selling to Men, Selling to Women* has been about gender differences and communication skills for salespeople. We've discussed process and planning skills, we've looked at areas of possible blind spots for both genders, and we've introduced a new model of relational selling. As with most books, we've saved the best for last: a tool that taps contemporary business thinking on differences between people... and customers.

My current work in diversity strategy and education means exploration on a very deep level of the notion of differences in the workplace: differences in thinking styles and personality, differences in age, race, gender, and sexual orientation, and differences in work styles and consumer equity.

The end result of an effective diversity strategy is to leverage these differences for bottom line results and competitive advantage in the marketplace. In a significant amount of diversity education, we talk about race and gender and biases that may exist. As long as labels exist for groups of people, some amount of bias will be present. To test this, try this simple exercise.

> Bias, what bias?
> Ask some of your friends to pick a common label for a group of people in the workplace. Let's say, female managers, then ask, "What are some of the negative things other people say about this group?"

Bias, what bias? (con't)
Invariably, you will get answers like; bitchy, controlling, indecisive, talk too much, too soft, chatty, etc. After you get a list of 10 to 15 items; ask the question, 'Is it fair to say that we have heard these things said by other people?' (Yes). And, is it fair to say that much of society believes these things to some level? (Yes). And, is it fair to say that all of us are a representation of society? (Yes). Then, is it fair to say that at some level we may in fact have some of these beliefs ourselves? (After much silence, you will usually get a weak, yes, from some honest soul.)

If we are human, we have some preconceived notions about people, and about each other, men and women. The EVOVLE Tool will give us a mental model to not pre-judge, not jump to conclusions and allow us to genuinely value the person, which will let us build a relationship and truly value our customer.

The EVOLVE Tool is a mental six-point check list to allow you to:

- Dial down your bias toward the opposite gender.

- Genuinely value the customer.

- Remain open minded to all data being shared with you by the customer.

- Listen for facts and feelings.

- Validate what is truly important to the customer.

- Prepare a response appropriate for the customer.

Selling to Men Selling to Women

It should be noted that this is a check list and not a sequential model. You may end up using just one piece of the tool or you may end up using all of it.

To repeat and to help us remember the basic premise of the tool, the purpose is to remind you to eliminate bias, to genuinely value the person, to remain open minded, listen attentively, validate facts, and prepare an appropriate response. These are all things you should be doing all of the time anyway, and hopefully this tool reminds you to do one or all during every step of the selling process.

The EVOLVE Tool

E Explore Personal Bias

V Genuinely Value the Person

O Remain Open Minded

L Listen with a Male & Female Ear

V Prepare to Validate Facts

E Engage/Empathize

The EVOLVE Tool can be used during any step of the Evolved Selling Model. It is an important tool in planning, conducting the sale and building on-going relationships. In fact, once you become aware of the usefulness of the EVOLVE Tool, you may end up using it literally dozens of times during an actual sales cycle. To begin, let's take a closer look at that challenging first step.

Checkpoint #1: Explore Personal Bias

Bias in today's world has taken on a negative, almost criminal connotation, but Webster's definition is fairly mild:

Bias: *a temperamental or emotional leaning to one side.*

If we use this as our definition, it is easy to see how this applies to gender bias and how it could play out in selling. Defined this way, we can see that we all have biases.

We learned in Chapter 2 that many of the things we believe intuitively about gender are true. Many times the differences have a physiological or psychological basis, and because of this it is very easy for us to have gender bias in the sales process. If we go into a selling situation with a female, and we know she is processing more data or seeking validation, we can then use this to better understand her. If we are selling to a man, we need to ask ourselves, "What bias towards this person am I aware of within myself?" Understanding gender and the possible biases we may have becomes a strength rather than a weakness.

To understand the biases you may have, let's repeat our 'Bias, what Bias?' Exercise from above. In the box below, fill in your gender and then fill in the opposite gender. Then very quickly brainstorm a list of 20 words that come into your head. Do it quickly and don't judge or filter -- just write.

I am a _____, thinking about _____.

A form filled out by a colleague looked like this:

I am a <u>Woman</u>, thinking about a <u>Man</u>.

Big	Political	Build Stuff	Brad Pitt	Move Furniture
Likes Cars	Competitive	Loud	Mean	Cute
Teasing	Cook For	Helpful	Annoying	Smart
Boy Friend	Computers	Sports	Doesn't Listen	Matt LeBlanc

Based on this simple exercise, what do you notice? Perhaps that some words are positive and some are negative. The young woman who filled out this form had only been out of college for a few years and was in the advertising field, and perhaps because of that many of her words focused on the personal side of her life. It would in fact be virtually impossible to see a form filled out in exactly the same way for any two people. We are all different and unique in our experience and attitudes.

Let's take a look at your form. For the sake of this exercise, and for your own work, I would ask you to focus on the two or three most negative words, and the two or three most positive words. The words should be examined to understand if you have any bias against the other person that might surface subconsciously during the sales presentation.

Let's explore the trainee's negative words as an example. If she has even minor preconceived notions that men are loud, don't listen, and are political, these are almost certain to come into her head during a sales presentation and she might even take some action regarding them.

These counter productive beliefs could play themselves out like this:

Sub Conscious Bias	How I react when I am faced with that behavior	How the customer may react to my reaction
Men are Loud	I may retreat	Customer may see weakness and attempt to take advantage of the situation
	I may raise my voice	Customer may feel the need to be defensive and put up false objections
	I do not let it affect me; I stay calm in the moment and seek more understanding	Customer remains calm

What this says is that our beliefs and biases have an impact on our attitudes and actions. If we then take actions on these beliefs, we obtain results based on our beliefs and attitudes.

THE BELIEFS CYCLE

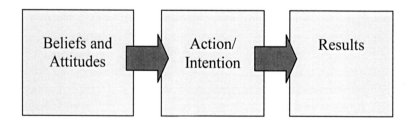

Adapted from ***Introducing Social Psychology***, Colin Fraser and Brendan Burchell, eds., Blackwell Pub., UK, 2001.

It is easy to see how our beliefs and biases could derail us in the selling process. This is all about how we treat people. It is natural, it happens everyday, and it is a big blind spot for most salespeople. This checkpoint requires self-awareness and it is an important step in every step of the selling process. It is especially important in the planning phase as it allows us time to think about our responses to situations, so that we are prepared rather than reactive in the moment.

We have looked at the negative side of bias, but let's explore what we would initially classify as neutral or positive thoughts. Let's go back to our young sales rep's list and examine cute, smart, Brad Pitt. These are obviously not negative thoughts. If we go back to our definition of bias as a temperamental or emotional leaning to one side, we see that the definition still applies. The young woman clearly has positive emotions towards some men, or some aspects of a man.

As humans, we react to what we see. As I asked the sales rep how she thought these words might play out in the sales cycle, she bravely said that she treats customers she finds attractive differently from those she finds unattractive. She said, that as a single woman, she is always looking for a connection with customers and she recognized that, yes, she does judge people by their appearance and as a result treats them differently.

This is in fact not unusual with the opposite gender as well. On many occasions, too numerous to count, I have been waiting in a buyer's office and started talking to another salesman. The discussion might turn to the administrative assistant to the buyer, and the salesman next to me would say something like, "Boy, Becky sure looks great today." Sometimes the buyer that we were calling on was also female. If the salesman was already "checking out" the assistant prior to meeting with the buyer, he was obviously taking some of those biases regarding women into the call.

We are human beings, and we are sexual animals. We also are capable of judging and making choices. Therefore it is logical to assume that we may in fact have a bias towards or against someone we find attractive, or someone we find unattractive. These are natural responses. However, if we are to truly value our customers and what they are asking for, we need to be aware of our own biases. That is the purpose of the first "E" in the

EVOLVE Tool. It might help us to uncover our own biases by asking a friend or colleague to assess our biases for us. Sometimes an objective third person can do a better job of giving us feedback than we can ourselves. And if we are not aware of our own personal biases, we can never move to Checkpoint 2, which is Genuinely Value the Person.

Checkpoint #2: Genuinely Value the Person

This step in the EVOLVE Tool really refers to the Action phase of the Beliefs Cycle. In the first 'E' step, Explore Gender Bias, we established that biases are present in our attitudes and beliefs. Once we are aware of bias, we can examine the intentions and resulting actions that come out of those biases. Once we are able to consciously dial down all of our biases, we will act in a non-judgmental, unbiased way. The outcome of this will be to Genuinely Value the Person to whom you are selling.

The focus of this second step in the EVOLVE Tool is significantly more applicable to men than to women. Time and time again when I ask women their biggest issue with being talked down to by men, the answer is, "I don't feel valued." Feeling valued is one of the core outcomes of positive relationships. The challenge for men is that we are often unaware we are devaluing women. This stems from not entirely understanding the way women speak.

Dr. Molly Epstein of Emory University in Atlanta refers to the style with which women communicate as Female Linguistic Patterns. Female Linguistic Patterns are groupings of words that are commonly used by females and fall into categories Epstein calls Disclaimers, Qualifiers, Hedges, and Tag Questions.

Let's examine what these look like:

Disclaimers start with:
> *"I'm not sure about this…"*
> *"This may not work, but…"*
> *"Correct me if I'm wrong, but…"*
> *"This may be a silly question, but…"*

Qualifiers are phrases like:

"*I think…*"
"*I feel…*"
"*I believe…*"
"*I imagine…*"

Hedges would sound like:

"*Sort of…*"
"*Perhaps…*"
"*Maybe…*"
"*What if we try…*"

And Tag Questions are those words seeking agreement, such as:

"*Okay?*"
"*Don't you agree?*"
"*Right?*"
"*You know?*"

While these statements are common to women and actually support the relationships that they enjoy, men often misinterpret these statements as being weak or non-committal. Women don't see them as that. They see them as a supportive part of valuing the listener over the speaker.

Many salesmen need to remember that these linguistic patterns are meant to create a connection and lessen tension between speakers. What they do not do is indicate the speaker's weakness or deep doubt. Women use emotion-filled words, like "I feel", to increase trust and openness between speakers. They use tag questions like "you know?" to create equality. These are bonding words, not indicative of inferiority. In response to these phrases or questions, therefore, the salesperson needs to, first, listen without judgment, nod affirmatively, and then respond to any concerns voiced in a non-patronizing way.

It's easy to see how we can easily devalue the female customer or what she is saying. Let's link this to our "E" on Explore Personal Bias. If we subconsciously think that women are indecisive, and then we hear words in the communication process that are non-committal, it is very easy for this judgment to become self-reinforcing. I thought it, I observed it, so it must be true -- when in fact, it is none of the above. It is just another way of communicating that we misinterpret.

This takes us to the next checkpoint in our model.

Checkpoint #3: Remain Open Minded

In all honesty, it is nearly impossible to remain completely open minded. This is what makes for good judges and therapists. It's also a trait that is important for every successful salesperson to work on, every single day. And it is at the heart of everything we have discussed in this book.

This step is designed to serve two different purposes. First, it links with Explore Personal Bias and Genuinely Value the Person to remind us to keep our awareness high regarding gender differences that might be present in our subconscious, but it also serves to help us pause for a moment to be aware of the buyer's role.

At the risk of sounding repetitious, women tend to be relational and men tend to be transactional. However, there are always exceptions, and this checkpoint is designed as a reminder that this maxim is not always true. By remaining open minded, we can step away from stereotyping our buyer and allow him or her to migrate back and forth between traditional roles. We can remain open to all possible options that might present themselves.

By remaining open minded, we can remind ourselves that the woman we are trying to sell to might only want to buy something and move on. It also allows us to be aware of men that want to build a relational partnership with our company or us. This flexibility is incredibly important in business today. It governs sales to our gender opposites, as well as to people who are minorities, gay, elderly, or disabled.

All long-term sales relationships have to be based on trust, respect and credibility. This is the essence of our Evolved Selling Model. When my company is selected as a strategic partner for a multi-year commitment, I am representing my company in building a relationship. My company's role is to understand their business, their processes, and the very culture of their company.

It's easier to preach open mindedness than practice it. If you think this is an area where you need help, I would suggest that you take a leadership development program that gives you 360-degree feedback from your peers and customers. This will allow you to get objective feedback about your own behaviors and actions as seen by others.

I would also recommend that you consciously practice a form of mind control, where you put all of your biases into a suitcase that you put away, leaving you with an uncluttered, open mind as you communicate with your buyer. It takes many, many practice sessions to achieve absolute open mindedness, but it is doable. It's also going to become absolutely necessary for the sales professional in this constantly changing sales landscape.

Checkpoint #4: Listen with Male and Female Ear

Many books and seminars have been written about listening and listening skills, and countless jokes have been written about men's inability to listen. As we said earlier in the book, it's not that men don't listen; they are just more keenly focused on something else. It is this ability to focus that may actually make men better listeners than women. They just need to choose to really focus their attention on listening to the person in front of them, not to the stuff that's running through their minds or to the newspaper they're reading.

So as to not introduce new stages and steps, I will place the three types of listening into our existing three sales models we've already discussed. We will call our three stages:

- **Transactional Listening**
- **Relational Listening**
- **Evolved Listening**

This is not only an appropriate way to think about listening skills, but it demonstrates how listening weaknesses may play out in the sales process.

Transactional Listening

Like most components of the transactional process, the focus is on the salesperson, but it also applies to listening. Transactional Listening is what many salespeople engage in on a daily basis. The salesperson is hearing words but they are not connecting at all. He or she is keenly focused on their solution, not the customer's. We saw this play out in Dave's talking over Rick's objection in our men's Tupperware party. This reflects an inward focus on the salesperson and his/her solution, not the customer. When I was selling paper products for Procter & Gamble, it was about selling my solution (a paper towel end-cap display) to my problem (i.e., selling end-cap displays). I wasn't really listening to the store owner's concern over margin and profitability.

This tendency of not listening is not only applicable to men. Female salespeople are often the worst people in the world when it comes to listening to men. Just as a male salesperson thinks they know what's right for a woman, so too do women think they know what's right for a man.

In my sales career I have moved more than ten times. My wife and I have the process down. I go to the next city and look for housing. I know exactly what she is looking for after this many moves. My process is to find a realtor, and tell them (usually a female), that I want to look at 100 different houses in our price range. From there I will pick ten to show to my wife when she comes into town. Now I have to tell you that the real estate lady laughs and says, *"You don't really want to see a hundred houses,"* but humors me and we start on our rounds.

After seeing about 30 homes in two days, she says, *"Aren't you getting confused by all these homes?"* and I say, *"No, I have only seen three that my wife would be interested in and I have taken notes on those. As I said, I want to see a hundred houses."* After two days, she has finally listened to me! Now I have to tell you that when we met, she did a thorough need assessment, (How many children do you have? What type of schools do you want? How many bedrooms? etc.). But even after an hour together assessing my needs and two days together in a car, it took this long to finally sink in! Our tendency as people, let alone as salespeople, is to be inwardly focused. It is only once you can stop thinking about yourself and start listening to the buyer that you will truly be successful.

Relational Listening

Relational Listening is focused on the feelings and connections with the buyer: the buyer's issues, the buyer's needs, the buyer's concerns. What does Relational Listening feel like?

The way to listen at a relational level is to turn off "the little voice inside your head." And in case you don't know what little voice that is, it's the one that just said to you, "What little voice?"

Turning off "the little voice inside your head" is the key to focusing on the other person. This is incredibly hard for salespeople, and I will tell you it is my greatest weakness. It is an area that I consciously struggle with and I am only now winning the battle. As a salesperson, you are always listening to connect your product or solution to your issue. You always want to be one step ahead of the customer. While listening (or pretending to listen) for customer needs, you may have a mental checklist going on inside of your head that looks like this:

- *My product does that.*
- *Hmm… sounds like a competitor has been in talking to my buyer.*
- *I can beat that price.*
- *Wow, that delivery date might be challenging.*
- *Even though you are listening, you may be listening selectively to what you can do to solve the problem. You must turn off all of these voices, to truly hear what the customer wants.*

While only you can tell what is going on in your head, you can see some signs of non-verbal cues if a salesperson is truly listening.

Relational Listening has some of the following components:
- *Strong eye contact.*
- *Salesperson's body may lean in slightly toward the customer.*
- *Head nods in agreement.*

And while you should turn off the little voice in your head regarding your product and solution, in Relational Listening you should be listening to your little voice for relational connections. These are the keys to determine if a customer is in fact interested in deepening the relationship with you or if this is truly a transactional situation. This is listening for more than words, it is listening for connection points in the relationship between your company and solution and the buyer's need.

In a business setting this might sound like, "our long-term plan is" or "our strategic vision is." In a non-business setting, it may sound like some of the statements we've heard before in Genuinely Value the Person.

"I think.."
"I feel…"
"I believe…"
"I imagine..."

These are connection phrases which we have said before may not be valued unless you know what you are listening for. By Relational Listening, you are not discounting these terms but valuing them as connection points.

Relational Listening develops from asking good questions and then valuing the answer. Our goal in listening is to move out of Transactional Listening into Relational Listening and then to move to stage three, which is Evolved Listening.

Evolved Listening

I describe Evolved Listening as listening with a male and female ear. Evolved Listening is listening with energy, emotion, and empathy. Evolved Listening is very strong in the non-verbal skills discussed in Relational Listening. You can see the energy the salesperson is emitting when listening. You see emotion in their non-verbal response and you literally see empathy in their eyes. You have truly connected with the customer on a very emotional level. This we would say is listening with the female ear. You are listening and connecting to the feelings of the words being spoken by the person.

The analogy I use is of someone relating a sad story about a situation in their life, possibly the passing of a loved one after a long terminal disease. As you listen to the story, you are drawn into the emotions of the person telling the story. You witness not only the person's emotions showing but also feel your own emotions. As a salesperson, if you can truly connect your feelings to the customer's, you will be perfectly aligned with their issues and their solutions. Listening with the female ear is all about empathy.

I use the term listen with a male ear to allow you to listen for facts and data behind the emotion. And as opposed to Transactional Listening, you are not judging or thinking of solutions; you are merely listening for the facts behind the situation. Evolved Listening uses all of the tools of Relational Listening and totally turns off the transactional, self-centered approach. This will allow you to get both the facts and the feelings behind the situation.

Listening with a male and female ear, the fourth checkpoint of the EVOLVE Tool, will be used extensively during Steps 2 through 5 of the Evolved Selling Model and, like all components of the EVOLVE Tool, it is an internal tool to help you to stay focused and non-biased in the sales situation.

The first steps of the EVOLVE Tool have focused on gathering information. The last two letters will allow us to begin to mentally prepare to share information with the buyer.

Checkpoint #5: Prepare to Validate

Up until now, we have focused on remaining non-judgmental. We have dialed down our gender bias; we have truly valued the person; we have managed to stay open-minded and we have listened attentively. It is now time to formulate a response, processing everything we've taken in.

Unfortunately, what usually happens next is a statement from the salesperson that sounds something like:

"I understand what you have been saying. Let me tell you how my product can uniquely fulfill your needs."

The purpose of the Prepare to Validate checkpoint is not for you to begin spewing all of your great knowledge at the customer. The purpose is to prepare you to ask for more information to help you understand the customer better. This second "V" of the EVOLVE Tool is to assist you in prioritizing the information that has been shared with you by the customer.

As with all of the EVOLVE Tool checkpoints, this is an internal process. Prepare to Validate is designed to remind you that the first response you should make is a non-judgmental reply to allow you to validate the information that has been shared. When applying Prepare to Validate, all you are doing is reminding yourself not to SELL but to SEEK greater understanding and not jump to conclusions.

It is easy to confuse this step with resolving issues or handling objections, as it is often seen as the transmission of data back to the buyer. Remember the EVOLVE Tool is the stuff that's going on inside your head. Your actual reply may look like paraphrasing or summarizing the information back to the customer, but that is merely the outward expression of what's going on inside your head. Let's revisit our home-buying situation from above to demonstrate.

In the situation with my real estate saleswoman, validating would have sounded like this at the initial meeting:

"Mr. Halter, you have mentioned that you are looking for a two-story colonial with four bedrooms, that is less than five years old. You want a large yard, in a good school district. You know exactly what type of house you and your wife would be interested in. You want to see 100 different homes, so that you can provide your wife with a list of the top ten that fit your criteria. What other considerations should I be aware of that I haven't mentioned?"

As you can see, she has played back to me everything I am looking for. What she is doing is Identifying Customer Needs (from the Evolved Selling Model). But prior to that, in her head, she reminded herself to not come out with a solution, but with a request for validation. This is the verbal expression of her mental model. This short but critical checkpoint allows you to set the stage to gather more information from the customer by reminding you not to come out with your solution, but to validate the facts in a non-judgmental manner.

This illustration is also a good example of the power of the EVOLVE Tool. If my last saleswoman was used to selling to only women, she may have had to Explore Personal Bias. After getting to know her, I believe that this was not an issue, and she worked successfully with many male clients. I also believe that I was Genuinely Valued and that this was not an issue either. What she had was a huge blind spot around being Open-minded. She had never had a client that wanted to see 100 homes, and it was hard for her to believe that that is what I wanted. She also never really got past Relational Listening. If she had, she would have known that I was sincere and she would then be open to finding my unique solution. Were gender issues involved? It's hard to say. But what it does demonstrate is that we all have blind spots in selling situations, and if we have a simple checklist to help us through it, it will make us much more successful.

Finally, this illustration shows that not every point in the checklist needs to be applied in every situation. If we quickly review each point mentally for applicability in every situation, we shouldn't have any blind spots arise in our sale.

Checkpoint #6: Engage/Empathize

Our final "E" is a double pneumonic, Engage/Empathize. The purpose of the last letter in the EVOLVE Tool is to begin to prepare you to dialogue with the customer. Once again it is an internal mental model that allows you to check your own tendencies and blindspots. It is designed to help you, in the moment, to remember to tailor your approach to the buyer.

What it means is that:

- If you are a man selling to a woman, check that you may have a blind spot regarding the ability to empathize with your buyer.
- If you are a woman selling to a man, check that you may have a blind spot regarding the ability to engage with your buyer.

For men, this can be extremely challenging. We call it using the F-word (not the bad one). The F-word I am referring to is feelings. If you are selling effectively to women you know how valuable this is. As our research has said, feelings and connectivity are critical components of a relationship. This last step is to prepare you to increase your empathy for your buyer. If you are listening at an Evolved level, this is very easy. You will see it and sense it. It sounds exactly like it feels:

"Daphne, I'm sensing that you don't feel comfortable with the solution we've discussed."

This statement may come out during the Resolve Issues step. The critical point was that the salesman was remembering to think about feeling and empathy before he asked the question. Asking questions about feelings drives connectivity and demonstrates your support of the relationship, even though this may be the toughest task a salesman may have to do.

For women selling to men, this is a reminder not to empathize. If you have examined your own bias, beliefs and style, you know if this is an issue for you. This quick check is to remind you not to be indirect in your approach, but to be straightforward in your next step.

Just as a man may want to address the issue directly, if we reexamine female linguistic patterns, we are reminded that you may begin your questioning process with:

"I think..."
"I feel..."
"I believe..."
"I imagine..."

By remembering Engage, you will minimize your tendency to empathize and will provide a more powerful and direct reply to your buyer. Let's reexamine our real estate saleswoman.

The Validate Facts statement from above was:

"Mr. Halter, you have mentioned that you are looking for a two-story colonial with four bedrooms, that is less than 5 years old. You want a large yard, in a good school district. You know exactly what type of house you and your wife would be interested in. You are interested in seeing 100 different homes, so that you can provide your wife with a list of the top ten that fit your criteria. What other considerations should I be aware of that I haven't mentioned?"

It is engaging, unemotional and direct. Now read the same example with a softer touch, containing female linguistic patterns:

"Mr. Halter, I think that you are looking for a two-story colonial with four bedrooms, that is less than 5 years old. I'm imagining a large yard, with a good school district. I feel you know exactly what type of house you and your wife would be interested in. I believe you are interested in seeing 100 different homes so that you can provide your wife with a list of the top ten that fit your criteria. Have I forgotten anything? What other considerations should I be aware of that I haven't mentioned?"

You will notice that the changes are minor. You may even say, "What's the big deal?"

Well, if you are a woman selling to a man, the potential exists for this softer version to reinforce any bias that I have toward women, and place you in a less than equitable position with me, the male buyer. When it comes to negotiating the price of the house, do you think that I will value your judgment? Or pass you off as some too-soft saleswoman?

Remember, everything communicates. In a business related situation, given this soft speak, I may not really value your solution and may shut you down as not really understanding what I need in a product or a solution.

This "E" links very closely with Prepare to Validate Facts, in regards to giving information back to the customer. As with that "V", it is not what you are saying, but what you are planning on saying. It's designed to help you think ahead.

All of the checkpoints of the EVOLVE Tool are designed to help you, in the moment, to check your own biases, weaknesses and blind spots. In our next chapter we will explore how the Evolved Selling Model and the EVOLVE Tool work together to create the Evolved Selling Process.

LEARNINGS FROM THIS CHAPTER

1. Our personal beliefs and biases can derail us when we sell, and the savvy salesperson needs a tool to remind her or him of those negatives and of the positives that should replace them.

2. The EVOLVE Tool serves as a reminder for gender-aware behaviors that are appropriate for the salesperson before, during and after the sale.

3. E = Explore Personal Bias.

4. V = Genuinely Value the Person.

5. O = Remain Open Minded.

6. L = Listen with a Male and Female Ear.

7. V = Prepare to Validate.

8. E = Engage/Empathize with your buyer, depending on whether he or she is a transactional or relational buyer.

Chapter 10
The Evolved Selling Model

> It is not the strongest of the species that survive, or the most intelligent, but the most responsive to change.
>
> - Charles Darwin

The Evolved Selling Model is simple in that it is spatially related to the familiar transactional model, but it's organic in design, constantly flowing in a circular format. In other words, it is user friendly to both genders. It allows for the need to visualize a structured process while allowing for relational connections at several points. The Evolved Selling Model provides the structure and framework for the entire sales process. When used with the EVOLVE Tool, it becomes a process built for success that identifies any gender issues that might present themselves. The Evolved Selling Model can be used by people who are new to sales, or it can be adapted by sales professionals.

Since this book is written for the latter group, I am not going to spend a lot of time here talking about what is going on at each step. In Chapter 11 we will get into application exercises and take a deep dive into what is going on in each step.

As a sales professional, my hope is that you will use this structure to sequence your existing skills. If you are not doing one of the steps or want to work on it more, you will get the chance to do so in Chapter 11. However, because the premise of this book is gender differences, I want to explain step by step how gender differences may play out during each stage of the model and help you identify potential issues that may be present.

I will revisit the stages of the Model and examine some potential gender blind spots that all salespeople need to be aware of at every checkpoint of the process. I'll offer some insights about gender differences that the sales professional needs to remember, insights that might prevent him or her from losing the sale. Also I'll keep reminding you that not every male or female is typical of that gender, but there are enough commonalities to make some generalizations.

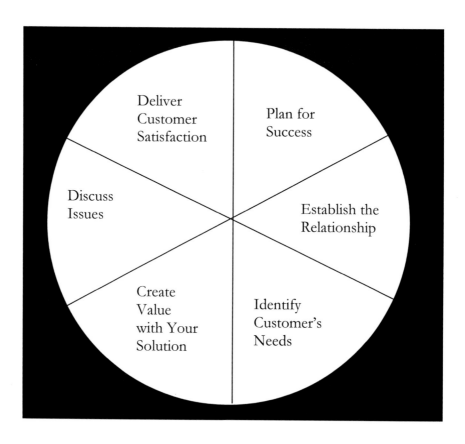

Blind Spots in Planning for Success

- When salespeople talk about planning the sale, even when they use a mapping process, they seldom consider planning to gender, or taking the buyer's gender into consideration. In our Model, the salesperson always prepares mentally for the gender that he or she could encounter. Any mapping process should indicate gender and should remind you to plan accordingly. You should use the EVOLVE Tool extensively during this time to identify blind spots in your planned approach.

- If you have identified that gender differences may be present, educate yourself about those differences. Reading this book is a start. Doing the Try This On exercises is a good second step. Next, do some research. Just as you wouldn't walk into a customer blindly, my hope is that you have figured out that, yes, gender matters and there are a lot of resources to help you. There is a list of books on gender and selling in the Bibliography. Read them and learn.

- Observe the differences between men and women you see around you during your day. Talk to successful salesmen who sell to women, and find out what their secrets are. Talk to successful women who sell to men. Talk to your co-workers. If you genuinely want to know what's going on from a gender perspective, ask your co-workers about some of their largest recent purchases. Then ask them if any gender issues were present.

- If you are calling on customers for the first time, hopefully through the appointment process you have determined the gender of the buyer. The watch-out here is even if you planned for "Mrs. Wilson", don't assume she wants a relationship with you or your company. Apply the EVOLVE Tool early on.

- Plan your first few minutes very carefully. How will you show genuine interest? What bias might be present? Remember that the first seconds leave a lasting impression on your buyer. To women, attitude and non-verbals are extremely important, no matter how attractive the product qualities and price. Salesmen who approach a female buyer looking casual or disengaged will turn off the buyer. Get feedback from a trusted female colleague or better yet rehearse your opening with her. Then listen carefully to her feedback.

- For the male buyer, remember the product may be more important than the salesperson. To sell to most men you have to know your product inside out. Men are impressed by knowledge about data and facts. Do your homework, ladies! Be prepared to answer every question. Get a male colleague to question you as a male buyer would.

- If you are selling to men and women at the same time, decide on your plan for connecting with both of them. Practice the art of switching between male and female buying influences. Since relationships take longer to form, plan places in your presentation for relational questions and plan for fact-based situations to arise.

Blind Spots in Establishing the Relationship

- The biggest mistake salespeople make is jumping to conclusions early on in the call. Some of the first sales training I had taught me to look around the office and ask about family pictures, or golfing trophies. If you are doing this, you are jumping to conclusions and, as the Beliefs Cycle told us, the actions we take may be based on our beliefs and not the buyer's. Stay business focused and follow the buyer's lead. It won't take long to determine what's on the buyer's mind.

- Male sellers: be prepared to spend more time with most female buyers than with men. They want to get to know you. Those buyers want to know who YOU are. Can they trust you? Are you hearing them? Even when there's little time for interaction, it's vitally important for the salesman to connect with the average female buyer.

- It is imperative for male sellers to demonstrate to female buyers that they are respected, right from the beginning. It's my experience that the number one reason women turn down a salesman is because they felt they were not treated as an equal. This doesn't mean that the woman wants a glib, flattering sales pitch. Women have historically been treated so badly by salesmen that they are suspicious to begin with, and they prefer a more vulnerable, open approach by a male salesperson. Being too rehearsed can in fact be a negative.

- Male buyers, on the other hand, want to forego the let's-get-to-know-each-other dance, and go straight from the meeting and greeting into the product. Female salespeople need to remember that women communicate three times as much as men. Bring your communications level to him, and he'll appreciate it. One of the main gripes of male buyers is that saleswomen simply talk too much. Observe your male client and match his communication level and emotions.

- Over-familiarity is a turn-off for male buyers. Most men don't want to know much about you, unless they discover that you played sports with a professional team or can otherwise impress them. Ladies, the way to establish the relationship with your male buyer is to know your product, stick to the facts, and stay out of their personal business – until you know them better. Remember, they've had so much training about sexual harassment that they won't feel comfortable becoming too personal with you anyway.

- For women calling on men, if you sense they want a relationship find connection points that they are comfortable with. This may involve family, sports, money or business, but be cautious. If the buyer says his son plays soccer, that doesn't give you permission to talk about your son playing soccer. Stay focused on the customer and value him. While it is very natural for women to want to share, men don't have that urge. If the buyer asks, then go there slowly. Men like sound bites, not stories.

- And more on sports for saleswomen. I have been to sales seminars that teach women to "talk more like men," and the facilitators say that if you learn about sports you can connect better with men. I would tell you to be very cautious. As we have said in this book, men already have preconceived notions that minimize women. The watch-out is, if you don't know sports, really know sports, then don't go there. Just as women can see through men who aren't genuine, so can men. Does this mean women shouldn't talk sports? Absolutely not. But, if you can't compute an ERA (earned run average) or know the role of a weak-side linebacker, you hold the potential of costing yourself credibility with the buyer.

- For men selling to women, allow the woman to lead the way in establishing the relationship. Observe if she wants to connect or not. If she doesn't want a relationship, don't press. Be warm, but not overly enthusiastic. Women can see through pretense like nobody's business. Stay in the sincerity zone; and remember that some women are transactional buyers. Find out where your female buyer is. If she gives the signal that she wants to hear more, start the connection process. But before you give her your life story, demonstrate that you are a listener. A serious listener who hears HER. That adds huge value to her relationship-building process.

- For long-term sales, it is expected by both male and female buyers that they will get to know the seller on a more personal level, although women put more emphasis on this than men. Let your customers indicate how personal they are willing to get. Getting too personal too soon with some customers may turn them off forever. However, there are other customers who will eventually embrace you and see you as a partner rather than a salesperson. You want them to get to the point of seeing you on their side, rather than as a representative of your company. This means that you have to be honest at every level of the sale. Remember, most women can smell dishonesty.

- Selling to men and women at the same time and establishing a relationship with both can be tricky. The salesperson has to be able to connect with the female buyer, while respecting the male need for brevity and information. Switching back and forth satisfactorily takes skill, and should, as I've said, be practiced beforehand. Salesmen MUST demonstrate EQUAL respect for both the woman's and the man's opinion and needs. There are very few demure women left who will happily sit and be ignored. If she feels disrespected, she'll sink your sale. Allow time to connect to the woman relationally, while engaging the man in direct conversation and questioning.

- In the Building Relationship step, you will be using all of the components of the EVOLVE Tool.

Blind Spots in Identifying the Customer's Needs

- The style in which men and women identify their needs varies dramatically. Men tend to voice their own needs clearly. It's that compartmentalized brain focusing on the data. These are his needs, and his personal wins. Get his need identified and answered without elaboration. Get to the bottom line quickly. Saleswomen, you may need to keep your questions brief and to the point. Don't answer with long-winded stories.

- Female buyers may or may not know their actual needs. This is because they may be open to more than one solution. Salesmen often try to verbalize the needs of the female customer to the great irritation of the latter. Find out first what the buyer is seeking in a solution. Women are processing multiple data points and multiple solutions. She is looking for connection points of multiple solutions. You can guide her by asking questions that help her draw conclusions about the data she is taking in. Asking questions like, "Tell me more about your ideal solution" or "What would you imagine the ideal solution to be?" -- if asked with genuine respect -- can be very helpful in crafting a relationship and a solution.

- She may have done her research already and be very clear. If there is hesitation, then you need to apply the EVOLVE Tool. Being impatient with a female who is in doubt is a blind spot for many salesmen. Please understand that women think in a multitasking way, so while they are talking to you, they're thinking of many other needs that might be more important. They might be unsure of the need because they're considering that the price might be prohibitive or the appearance might not be suitable. Be patient. Get the full story behind the hesitation so you can move into the next stage.

- When selling to men and women at the same time, the salesperson has to clearly identify both sets of needs. Get the input of both by addressing questions to them in turn. For example, turn to the man and ask, "What do you have in mind in terms of your wife's life insurance needs?" Then turn to the woman and ask, "What do you have in mind...?" The next question should be addressed to the woman first. Allow equal time for eye contact, make notes equally, and prepare to identify their needs separately but equally, finding common ground with a win-win solution. In a business setting, when men and women are on the buying team, it must always be demonstrated that the females' opinions are as valuable as the male members'. Reference must be made to both genders' input and questions. The salesperson must keep reminding him/herself that the women value honesty and sincerity and the men want data.

- My strongest advice to salesmen selling to the female buyer is LEARN TO LISTEN. Use the EVOLVE Tool extensively. Value the Person, Remain Open-minded and Listen Effectively. Start practicing with your female colleagues and your significant other.

Blind Spots in Creating Value with Your Solution

Up until now in the Evolved Selling Process, we have been gathering information. We gathered information in Planning for Success. We spent significant time listening and inquiring in our next two steps to Establish the Relationship and Identify Customer Needs. It is now time to start sharing your thoughts on a solution.

This step comes over from the transactional step of Features, Advantages and Benefits, a very male-oriented model. By its nature this speaks of data and pleasure. As such, there are more blind spots for men selling to women than for women selling to men.

- For both female and male buyers, it's particularly important to show how you bring value, both through yourself as well as through the product. Salespeople have to be able to present accordingly, knowing that women may need the sales chemistry (i.e. relationship), but men may want to take charge of the purchasing process.

- Creating Value means giving both exactly the sales experience they need. Men want to know that your product is the right price and has the necessary qualifications. Women, this means that you find out what creates value for that male buyer, and sell them with exact, concise information. If he's buying a car and wants luxury plus durability, go straight to those two points. Give him enough data to convince him. If you have printed material to back you up, supply it there and then. Make your case and make it to order. No trimmings.

- Women, on the other hand, want to know that, despite all their doubts, they are not going to regret buying your product or service. Because of all their cross-brain wiring, women become more emotional during the buying process than men. That's how they become brand loyal. The best salesman is the one who eliminates all doubts for the female buyer, as this will make her comfortable with her decision. She wants to know that she's doing the right thing. Once he's done that well, she'll be back over and over again, because she's convinced she's getting value.

- Not only will a woman come back, but if she's convinced by your solutions, she will sell others on it. Women make it easy for the salesperson to sell through others so make sure that your female customer has all the information she needs and gets all her questions answered. She's becoming a gatherer-salesperson for you!

- The watch-out here for selling to men and women simultaneously is the same one we have mentioned before. Be sure to manage the needs of both buyers. He may want lots of facts and data (features and advantages). Keep checking in with the female buyer, to make sure she isn't getting bored or feeling isolated. Remember, she is creating value for the entire solution and she wants to know that she's doing the right thing, not just buying something.

Again, while the whole EVOLVE Tool may be used, Prepare to Validate Facts and Engage/Empathize are most often always applied in this step of Creating Value with Your Solution.

Blind Spots in Discussing Issues

If you have been successful in the previous steps, then the issues to be resolved are nothing more than unanswered questions. Delivery time and payment terms are possible issues that may arise. A key distinction at this step versus our transactional model is that you are not handling objections. If you have followed every step properly, real issues should be at a minimum. As issues arise, apply the EVOLVE Tool. Possible blind spots include:

- Selling to Men. Men sometimes just enjoy debating and may even be raising an issue to merely test your mettle. It has to do with testosterone. It's actually the start of male bonding. So let them bring up their concerns, even if they appear to be arguing with you, and then you should get down to business quickly and firmly giving your solutions. They'll respect you for that.

- To a woman, "No" means NO. This is because in her mind she has exhausted every solution. Women often don't realize that when a man says, No, it is not absolute. Given that he is fact based, if you can bring in new facts you are opening the door to allow room for change. Come back with another solution, and you'll have his ear.

- Non-verbal cues are very important at this stage. For women selling to men, being sensitive to a man's facial expressions and body language can give you a world of information about his thoughts. If he's holding a closed position, arms folded, eyes averted, there's a problem that's not being addressed. It's important here to ask three questions to see where you're off track. These are:

  - What do you like about the product?
  - What do you not like?
  - What else do you need?

Even the most stoic man should be able to give you answers that will point the way. And, please, don't try to establish a relationship with this man. Just answer the concerns.

- Women are quite different here. Discussing issues is part of the female way of connecting with other people, and thereby feeling good about themselves. The danger for salesmen here is that they could downplay the discussion process by answering the objections too quickly or casually. Women may be tentative anyway about voicing disagreement. The male seller has to make it safe for her to voice her concerns.

- If a woman feels that she is being put down, ignored or patronized in any way, she will turn off the sale, no matter how attractive the product or price. Her need for respect is more important than any product! Showing respect for the issues she thinks are important, no matter how foolish they may seem to you, is the way to gain her respect. So check your biases, guys. You're going to have to get ready for women buying everything from iron ore to tractor-trailers. All salesmen, and particularly those who are unaccustomed to female buyers, need to think of these discussions as educating your female customer for future buying – from you!

- In selling to men and women at the same time, a little more time will be needed to discuss issues with the female buyer than the male. Try to balance this out so that you are answering the woman's issues concisely, not turning the man off with the details, while considering his need to get to the point quickly.

Blind Spots in Delivering Customer Satisfaction

In this next step you will be applying all the checkpoints of the EVOLVE Tool.

- Customer satisfaction means different things to different genders. The bottom-line is that all customers want to feel confident that they did the right thing. However, men tend to focus more on the short-term transaction. If you deliver satisfaction on this product, they're happy. They may or may not buy from you again, because they're looking at price, product and pleasure/performance, and if a competitor can beat you on those, you may lose the next sale. Female salespeople have to think of every sale to a man as a one-off event, and come back and do it all over again. It's the product, not the relationship, that's important to that buyer. So don't take it personally. He may like you, but he can shift allegiance at a moment's notice, with no regrets.

- Understanding that women are brand loyal and relationship oriented is the bottom line for male sales professionals. Think of it her way. As many things as she has to do every day, working at home and at work, a woman wants to be able to stick with a product, get to know one salesperson, and go on to the next task. She will spend more time getting to know you and your product, but next time she'll save time by coming back to you and your product. That's why it's essential that you deliver customer satisfaction. Women will not only buy your product over and over, but they'll recommend it to their friends. If you don't deliver satisfaction, she'll rule you out – forever. Don't forget, women have long, long memories.

- Check with the male/female buying team to see if both customers are satisfied with the product. She might be less willing to voice her dissatisfaction, since women hate to be seen as critics. He will probably be more inclined to express himself. Make sure that both are heard, particularly if you want to get into a long-term sales relationship with them.

The EVOLVE Tool may not be specifically used in this step. However, if you have a follow-up situation or problem to resolve, you may need to use any or all of it to deal with the customer's issues. Delivering Customer Satisfaction is the cornerstone of developing and building relationships in the current and in the future.

We have examined a new relational sales model. The model and steps are configured to work in building relationships with men and women. The power of the Evolved Selling Model is not necessarily the steps but what you are doing to manage your own blind spots during the process. We have seen when and where these issues may arise. Now let us examine the practical application of the EVOLVE Tool that will allow you to use the Evolved Selling Process to its maximum potential.

LEARNINGS FROM THIS CHAPTER

1. Although everyone has blind spots when it comes to communicating with the opposite gender, the key is your own awareness and how you deal with it.

2. In Planning for Success, the sales professional needs to be aware of the gender of the buyer and plan accordingly.

3. Common blind spots in Establishing the Relationship can be female sellers becoming over-familiar with the buyer and male sellers not allowing enough time for rapport.

4. While Identifying the Customer's Needs, it's important not to make assumptions. Asking good questions is always the smart thing for the seller to do.

5. In Creating Value, a seller has to show men that the product is the right price and has the necessary qualifications. Women want to be assured they won't regret buying.

6. In Discussing Issues, female salespeople need to remember that the male buyer might sound as if he's arguing, when in fact this is just a desire for more data. Male sellers have to use this step to connect more with their female buyer.

7. Delivering Customer Satisfaction means different things to different genders. Women are brand loyal if they're convinced they received good service; men will switch without guilt if the price or quality is better elsewhere.

Selling to Men Selling to Women

Chapter 11
The Evolved Selling Process – Tools and Application

> By taking responsibility to change yourself instead of waiting for others to change, you will feel and exercise your new power to create positive and supportive relationships.
> - John Gray, *Mars & Venus in the Workplace*

If location is the key to retail, the slogan for selling should be planning, planning, planning. That's why the first step in the Evolved Selling Model is called Planning for Success. Most salespeople use some type of call planning as one of their key tools to being successful. Our model utilizes call planning but also asks you to be ready with more than product specifications and deal sheets.

My goal is to help you to go beyond your normal success ratio in building relationships by anticipating gender-related issues that might be present. I will do this by having you plan to examine any gender bias that might arise during each step of the sales process. You will also use the EVOLVE Tool to help you plan for any of those blind spots that might pop up during the sales process.

There is no excuse for skipping the planning process. Remember, planning is what makes the difference between order takers and sales professionals.

In order to help you, I've included three forms at the end of this chapter, designed to guide you from beginning to end of the sales process. Each form contains a number of highly relevant questions that the sales professional needs to answer carefully in order to prepare for the sales call. This form includes blind spots that the salesperson needs to complete to stay mindful of during the sales process.

Form #1: The Evolved Selling Model Planning Form

This planning tool, completed prior to the call, takes the seller through the six steps in the Evolved Selling Model by asking questions that prepare him or her to meet the challenges along the way.

Plan for Success:
In this important first section of the planning form, the gender of the buyer is noted along with gender differences, and the relational or transactional nature of the sale.

Establish the Relationship:
The salesperson is alerted to consider the gender differences that might be involved in establishing the relationship with the customer.

Identify Customer Needs:
Once gender differences are noted, the salesperson lists the steps now called for in identifying the customer's needs.

Create Value with Your Solutions:
The basis for value and its link to the customer's needs are outlined here.

Discuss Issues:
The salesperson has to list any issues that can be anticipated, gender or otherwise, along with the solutions to those issues.

Deliver Customer Satisfaction:
Here the seller is asked to outline the steps regarding gender differences that he/she can use to plan for the follow-up call on the customer.

Evolved Selling Model Planning Form™

Account:_____ Date of Call:_____

What is the objective of the call and who is the buyer?

Plan for Success	What is the gender of the buyer? What gender differences may be present in the call? Do you anticipate a relational or transactional sale? What data do you have to support this belief?
Establish the Relationship	How do you anticipate gender differences being involved in establishing a relationship?
Identify Customers Needs	What steps regarding gender differences will you plan for in identifying customer needs?
Create Value with Your Solution	What is the basis for value? How does this link to customer needs?
Discuss Issues	What issues do you anticipate and how will you handle them? What gender differences may have an impact on resolving issues?
Deliver Customer Satisfaction	What gender differences do you need to be aware of to deliver customer satisfaction?

Download this form for free at www.ywomen.biz

Form #2: The EVOLVE Tool Planning Form

The second form should be completed before the sales call. This tool will keep gender differences on the salesperson's mind by asking questions that involve personal reflection and deep honesty. The questions follow the EVOLVE Tool format and ask questions that may arise from each letter of the Tool.

Explore Personal Bias:
To begin with, the seller is challenged to write down the thoughts or beliefs regarding the opposite gender that may come into their mind during the call.

Genuinely Value the Person:
Think about how you will value the buyer and demonstrate that value during the transaction.

Remain Open-Minded:
This is to remind the salesperson to stay open minded to all issues, concerns and information shared by the buyer.

Listen with a Male and Female Ear:
The salesperson has to describe what he or she will do to listen for facts, feelings and emotion.

Prepare to Validate Facts:
In order to build self discipline, the seller prepares here to seek more information rather than immediately starting to share their solution.

Engage/Empathize:
The last step is straight forward; what statements will you make as a man selling to a woman to demonstrate empathy, and if you are a women selling to a man, what statements are you going to make to engage the male buyer.

Once you become comfortable with the EVOLVE Tool, you may not need to complete this form for every call. The key is to be mindful during both the planning process and in the call itself.

The EVOLVE Tool Planning Form™

Explore Personal Bias	What thoughts or beliefs regarding the opposite gender may come into your mind during the call?
Genuinely Value the Person	What will you do to demonstrate this in the sales call?
Remain Open-Minded	What will you do to remain open-minded during the call?
Listen with a Male and Female Ear	How will you listen for facts, feelings and emotion?
Prepare to Validate Facts	How will you validate facts while managing any gender differences that may be present
Engage/Empathize	If you are a woman selling to a man, how will you demonstrate engagement with your buyer? If you are a man selling to a woman, how will you demonstrate empathy with your buyer?

Download this form for free at www.ywomen.biz

During the Call: Your Personal Blind Spots Check List

Blind spots are with us almost all the time. Make your own list of your personal blind spots. Ask colleagues and family members to contribute to the list. Then check the list before the sales call to remind yourself, and again after the call to see if you have forgotten your blind spots.

Although we discuss blind spots in more detail in Chapter 9, here are some reminders:

Research:
Don't assume anything based solely on gender. Do your homework about the buyer's gender, personality, and buying style if at all possible. Remember that she may be transactional and he may be relational.

Gestures:
Recall that women use three times the non-verbal gestures of men. Too much animation and use of non-verbals may make male buyers uncomfortable.

Time:
Men may want less time than women to establish a relationship.

Content:
Women may want more detail than men. Men may want more data.

Connection:
Find points of mutual interest when talking to men, but don't make it too obvious. It's more important for women buyers to find connections that make them feel comfortable.

Form #3: The Evolved Selling Call Follow-up Form

Once the call has been completed, it's time to analyze and plan for follow-up action. The Evolved Selling Call Follow-up form is designed to walk you step by step through that process of honest analysis. This is ideally used with a sales team or as a one on one review with the salesperson and the sales manager.

Plan for Success:
In this first section of the form, the sales professional is asked to plan for the next call. List what you learned about the buyer and the type of buyer it is (transactional/relational), and how will you use this knowledge on your next opportunity.

Establish the Relationship:
Gender differences noticeable during the relationship building process are then described. This is a particularly useful section, because certain patterns in communication come clear at this point.

Identify Customer Needs:
Customer needs are then put into the context of gender differences.

Create Value with Your Solution:
Examine the basis for value and capture how the customer responded to your solution. Again, did you notice anything regarding gender differences?

Discuss Issues:
Issues are looked at in two ways here: first, general issues that arose during the call, and second, issues that were a result of gender differences.

Deliver Customer Satisfaction:
In this last step, the salesperson notes lessons learned about gender differences that will be planned for in the next call on the customer.

Evolved Selling Call Follow-Up Form™

Account:_____ Date of Call:_____	
Plan for Success	Building on your success, what will you plan to do again on your next call? What area of opportunity can you plan better for next time?
Establish the Relationship	In establishing the relationship, what did you do/notice regarding gender differences?
Identify Customers Needs	In identifying customer needs, what did you do/notice regarding gender differences?
Create Value with your Solution	What was your basis for value? How did the customer respond to the solution? Did you notice anything regarding gender differences?
Discuss Issues	What issues arose and how did you handle them? Do you think gender differences had an impact on resolving the issues?
Deliver Customer Satisfaction	What steps regarding gender differences will you take away and plan for in your next call on this customer?

Download this form for free at www.ywomen.biz

Chapter 12
What's Next!

> "Old beliefs do not lead you to new Cheese."
> - Haw the Mouse, *Who Moved My Cheese*

In closing, every sales professional can become gender competent. Obviously, they will have to if they plan to continue selling. Women will have to sell to men more often as they rise through the ranks of the sales industry, and men will have to see their female sales customer as their equal. Every salesperson that wants to succeed in the future will have to accept two new facts.

First, the American market, like the rest of the world, is in the midst of a huge shift. We will see this in the work place and in the marketplace. The Perfect Storm is coming! The nature of sales is changing at a dizzying pace. Salespeople will need to evolve or they will become extinct. Order takers will be replaced by a microchip that is faster, cheaper and can be programmed to be adaptive to the purchaser's exact needs.

Second, there are differences between men and women that are not going to go away and that's quite frankly a good thing. Sales can be a very challenging career. Hopefully by now you have seen the impact that gender differences have in the sales area and you are well armed with the tools you need to be successful in Selling to Men and Selling to Women.

Finally, the very nature of business as we have known it for the past 40 years is going to be dramatically reshaped. In a few short years, New Millennium graduates will move into management ranks at all major companies. These are not bricks and mortar employees that desire corner offices, pension plans and seek lifetime benefits from companies. They are technically competent and may never work in a traditional office. They will be wired and mobile. Companies will be outsourcing more and contract work will soar for those people possessing the right skills. The ability to manage virtual, technically competent workforces will replace today's practices of how we manage people today. Organizations that are inflexible, authoritative and driven from the top will wake up in a few years and not have any capable workers to draw from.

Successful organizations will need managers and salespeople who genuinely value employees, are adaptable and can build conscientious, will genuinely listen and understand people's issues, and finally empathize with all of the change going on around them. As this book is around gender differences, some may even say that these skills are more closely feminine than masculine traits. If you believe that then you need to reread the book.

Great management, just like great sales ability is not gender biased, only people are.

BIBLIOGRAPHY

Mitch Anthony, *Selling with Emotional Intelligence*, Dearborn Trade, 2003.

Mary Kay Ash, *Mary Kay: The Success Story of America's Most Dynamic Businesswoman*, Harper & Row, NY, 1981.

Linda Babcock and Sara Laschever, *Women Don't Ask: Negotiation and the Gender Divide*, Princeton University Press, NJ, 2003.

Bill Bachrach, *Values-Based Selling: The Art of Building High-Trust Client Relationships*, Aim High Publishing, San Diego, CA, 1996.

Terry Burnham and Jay Phelan, *Mean Genes: Taming Our Primal Instincts*, Penguin Books, NY, 2001.

Jack Carew, *You'll Never Get No for an Answer*, Pocket Books, NY, 1987.

Jim Cathcart, *Relationship Selling: The Key to Getting and Keeping Customers*, HDL Publishing Co., 1987.

Jim Cathcart, *The Eight Competencies of Relationship Selling: How to Reach the Top 1% in Just 15 Extra Minutes a Day*, Leading Authorities, Washington, DC, 2002.

Colin Fraser and Brendan Burchell, *Introducing Social Psychology*, Blackwell Pub., UK, 2001.

Pamela Boucher Gilberd, *The Eleven Commandments of Wildly Successful Women*, McMillan Spectrum, NY, 1996.

Jeffrey Gitomer, *The Sales Bible*, William Morrow, NY, 1994.

John Gray, *Mars and Venus in the Workplace: A Practical Guide for Improving Communication and Getting Results at Work*, HarperCollins, NY, 2002.

Stephen E. Heiman and Diane Sanchez, *The New Strategic Selling*, Warner Books, NY, 1998.

Carole Hyatt, *The Woman's New Selling Game*, McGraw Hill, NY, 1998.

Spencer Johnson, *Who Moved My Cheese?*, G.P. Putman's Sons, NY 2002

Nicki Joy, *Selling is a Woman's Game: 15 Powerful Reasons Why Women Can Outsell Men*, Avon Books, NY, 1994.

Robert B. Miller and Stephen E. Heiman, *Conceptual Selling*, Henry Holt Pubs., NY, 1987.

Robert B. Miller and Stephen E. Heiman, *Strategic Selling: The Unique Sales System Proven Successful by America's Best Companies*, Warner Books, NY, 1985.

Anne and Bill Moir, *Why Men Don't Iron: The Fascinating and Unalterable Differences between Men and Women*, Kensington Publishing, NY, 1999.

Orv Owens, *The Psychology of Relationship Selling: Developing Repeat and Referral Business*, Lifetime Books, Hollywood, FL, 1996.

Jeanne Ellis Ormrod, *Human Learning*, Prentice Hall, NJ, 1995.

Barbara and Allan Pease, *Why Men Don't Listen and Women Can't Read Maps*, Broadway Books, NY, 1998.

Tom Peters, *The Circle of Innovation: You Can't Shrink Your Way to Greatness*, Vintage, NY, 1999.

Tom Peters, *Re-imagine! Business Excellence in a Disruptive Age*, Dorling Kindersley, London, UK, 2003.

Faith Popcorn and Lys Marigold, *Eveolution: The Eight Truths of Marketing to Women*, Hyperion, NY, 1998.

Neil Rackham, *Spin Selling*, McGraw Hill, NY, 1988.

Sharon Roberts, *Selling to Women and Couples: Secrets of Selling in the New Millennium*, Cambium Press, Plano, TX, 1995.

Gillian Royes and Candace Kaspers, *Sexcess: The New Gender Rules at Work*, Xlibris Pubs., PA, 2003.

Peggy J. Rudd, *Who's Really from Venus? The Tale of Two Genders*, PM Publishers, Texas, 1998.

Peter Senge, *The Fifth Discipline*, Currency Doubleday, NY, 1990.

Peter Senge, *The Fifth Discipline Fieldbook*, Currency Doubleday, NY, 1994.

Len Serafino, *Sales Talk: How to Power Up Sales Through Verbal Mastery*, Adams Media Corp., MA, 2003.

Jose Silva and Ed Jr. Bernd, *Sales Power: The Silva Mind Method for Sales Professionals*, Perigree, 1992.

Deborah Tannen, *Talking from 9 to 5: How Women's and Men's Conversational Styles Affect Who Gets Heard, Who Gets Credit, and What Gets Done at Work*, William Morrow, NY, 1994.

Judith C. Tingley and Lee Robert, *Gender Sell: How to Sell to the Opposite Sex*, Touchstone, NY, 1999.

Brian Tracy, *Be a Sales Superstar*, Berret-Koehler, 2002.

Julia Wood, *Gendered Lives: Communication, Gender and Culture*, Thomson Wadsworth, Belmont, CA, 2005.

Thomas Wood-Young, *Intuitive Selling: A Practical, Holistic Approach to Sales and Marketing that Gets Results*, WY Publishing, Colorado Springs, 2000.

Men and Women Communicate Differently
So What's the Big Deal for Salespeople?

The most significant variable in every sales situation is the gender of the buyer, more importantly, how the sales person communicates to the buyer's gender. It is now a validated and documented fact that men and women communicate differently, very differently. Everything from eye contact, to body language, to the usage of language and the processing of information is different in men and women.

What does this have to do with the Selling Process? Well, just about everything!

- Would you like to know more about this challenging topic?
- Is your company prepared for The Perfect Storm?
- Is your sales staff ready to compete in the 21st Century?

To learn more please go to: **www.ywomen.biz**

There you can find free downloads of the sales forms discussed in this book, arrange for quantity discounts on large book orders and find out more about bringing this information to your company.

Finally, now that you have read and used the techniques in *SELLING TO MEN, SELLING TO WOMEN* let us know what you think.

- Did it help you to close more business and improve relationships?
- Do you have an interesting story to share regarding gender differences?
- Do you have a success story that we can share with others, if so please let us know!

E-mail your comments to: **jthalter@ywomen.biz**

Jeffery Tobias Halter is a consultant, author, gender strategist and the President of YWomen, a strategic consulting company focused on engaging men in women's leadership issues. Jeffery is the former Director of Diversity Strategy at The Coca-Cola Company. In this role he managed the integration of the company's strategies regarding diversity and multiculturalism in relationship to the marketplace, the community and the workplace.

Jeffery is a Certified Trainer in Jack Carew's - Dimensions of Professional Selling; and Achieve Global's Genuine Leadership Series. He also holds certifications in HRM's Coaching and Feedback, DDI's Targeted Selection and Performance Management, Miller - Heiman's Strategic Selling and Conceptual Selling, and PDI's 360°` Feedback, and has worked in North America, Asia, Europe, and Africa. He is also a contributing author to Pink Magazine.

He has an Undergraduate Degree in Marketing from the University of Wisconsin and a Master of Science in Instructional Technology and Adult Education from Georgia State University. He has been an Instructor in Business Communications at Georgia State University and has also worked with the Graduate Communications Department at Emory University.

Gillian Royes has been an international communications manager, consultant and lecturer since 1979. She has worked in both the private and public sectors of the Caribbean and the United States, and has published two books to date. Her management experience includes being a division director of an airline and owning the largest craft distributing company in the Caribbean.

In the US, she has consulted to clients including Georgia Power, CB Richard Ellis, Medicare/Medicaid, and the Bureau of Alcohol, Tobacco and Firearms. Her most recent publication is entitled **Sexcess: The New Gender Rules at Work** (Xlibris Pubs., 2004).

Gillian's education includes an MA in Journalism from the University of Wisconsin, Madison, and a Ph.D. in Communications and History from Emory University, Atlanta, Georgia. She is a lecturer in Business Communications at the Robinson College of Business, Georgia State University.